INTRODUCTION TO COMPUTER–AIDED DRAFTING

INTRODUCTION TO COMPUTER-AIDED DRAFTING

David L. Goetsch

PRENTICE-HALL, INC. *Englewood Cliffs, New Jersey 07632*

Library of Congress Cataloging in Publication Data

Goetsch, David L.
 Introduction to computer-aided drafting.

 Includes index.
 1. Computer graphics. I. Title.
T385.G63 1983   604.2'4'02854   82-15016
ISBN 0-13-479287-4

Editorial/production supervision and
 interior design: Ellen Denning
Cover design: 20/20 Services, Inc.
Manufacturing buyer: Anthony Caruso
Page layout: Marie Alexander

Cover photograph courtesy of COMPUTERVISION Corporation.

PRENTICE-HALL INTERNATIONAL, INC., *London*
PRENTICE-HALL OF AUSTRALIA PTY. LIMITED, *Sydney*
EDITORA PRENTICE-HALL DO BRASIL, Ltda., *Rio de Janeiro*
PRENTICE-HALL CANADA INC., *Toronto*
PRENTICE-HALL OF INDIA PRIVATE LIMITED, *New Delhi*
PRENTICE-HALL OF JAPAN, INC., *Tokyo*
PRENTICE-HALL OF SOUTHEAST ASIA PTE. LTD., *Singapore*
WHITEHALL BOOKS LIMITED, *Wellington, New Zealand*

To Deborah M. Goetsch, Tom Seales, Phyllis Seal,
and all of the other drafting and design Students of
Okaloosa-Walton Junior College, past, present, and future.

CONTENTS

PREFACE

This book was written for the drafting, engineering, and construction student faced with the necessity of developing computer drafting skills. If not now, then in the foreseeable future, this will mean all drafting, engineering, and construction students. Computer-aided drafting is not a new drafting field. Rather, it is a new way to produce drawings in all traditional drafting fields.

Computer-aided drafting is being done by architectural, civil, mechanical, electronics, piping, and pictorial drafters as well as by drafters in virtually every other field. One does not simply take a course of study in computer-aided drafting and then become a computer drafting technician. Students must first learn all the background, theory, knowledge, design concepts, and skills of conventional drafting in the drafting field of their choice. Once a student knows how to do conventional drafting in a certain field, he or she can learn how to do the same type of drafting using the computer.

Introduction to Computer-Aided Drafting was written for the person who has already learned conventional drafting skills in his or her selected drafting field and must now learn how to perform his or her job using a computer drafting system instead of the traditional manual tools of the drafter. It is assumed that students using this textbook have no prior knowledge of computers.

Because many drafting engineering and construction students will have little or no knowledge of computers, the first three chapters have been provided to allow them to develop the working knowledge of computers necessary in order to understand computer drafting. In Chapter 1, students will learn about the different classifications and types of computers. They will also learn about the various components that make up a computer system and what each component contributes to the system. Chapter 1 concludes with a presentation of computer benefits and applications.

In Chapter 2, students will learn how human beings communicate with computers to make them work. Students will learn the various steps used to solve problems or perform tasks using a computer as a tool. They will also receive an overview of such computer programming tasks as systems flowcharting, program flowcharting, and BASIC language programming.

Chapter 3 covers computer-related math. All technical students learn a certain amount of math as it relates to their particular field. However, most drafters have had little or no exposure to computer-related math. Persons involved in computer drafting must be well versed in the mathematical concepts that relate to their field and with computer-related math. This chapter helps students fill in the gaps in their knowledge of computer-related math.

After completing Chapters 1 to 3, students will have a sufficient background in computers in general. They will then be prepared to learn the specific applications of the computer in drafting. Chapter 4 answers several questions people often ask about computer-aided drafting. It then illustrates the various ways in which the computer is being used as a tool in several different drafting fields.

Chapter 5 describes computer drafting systems and the individual components that make them up. In this chapter, students learn about the computer drafting hardware which replaces the conventional tools they have historically used when doing drafting manually. This chapter leads into Chapter 6, in which students learn how computer-aided drafting is actually done.

The final chapter covers employment in computer-aided drafting. This is an important chapter for drafting students because in addition to teaching job skills, today's drafting instructors must also teach students how to find, get, and keep a job in drafting. In modern education, a successful placement record is no longer a luxury, it is a necessity. In this chapter, drafting students learn how to prepare for the job search, how to identify potential employers of computer drafting technicians, how to get a job with one of these employers, and how to keep a job and advance in it after being hired. A comprehensive glossary of computer aided drafting terms follows Chapter 7.

Introduction to Computer-Aided Drafting is designed in such a way that it can be used for both traditional teaching settings and individualized, self-paced study. Each chapter contains: objectives; a heavily illustrated presentation of the material; a comprehensive summary and review; and a self-test so that students can measure their learning in each chapter before proceeding to the next chapter. It was written around the premise that all technical instructors in such areas as drafting, engineering, and construction should be teaching computer-aided drafting whether or not their school actually has a computer-aided drafting system.

The content and illustrations are presented in such a way that students can develop a good working knowledge of computer-aided drafting without the benefit of a computer-aided drafting system. Those instructors in schools that do have a system can take their students one step further and have them complete the computer-aided drafting exercises given in the appendix. Students who complete a thorough study of the material in this textbook will be well prepared to develop operational skills on the job if they do not have the opportunity to do so while in school.

All students beginning a study of computer-aided drafting should understand one principle from the outset. Drafting is still drafting, and it still serves the same purposes that it always has. Computer-aided drafting is not a new type of drafting — it is a new way to do drafting. Computers do not do drafting. People do drafting using the computer as a tool. Computer-aided drafting systems were not designed to replace people. They were designed to allow drafters to expand their capabilities, perform their work more efficiently, and complete more work in less time. The drafting, engineering, and construction student who learns to use the computer as a tool will be a much more productive person on the job. This textbook was designed to help students do just that.

DAVID L. GOETSCH

INTRODUCTION TO COMPUTER-AIDED DRAFTING

1

INTRODUCTION
TO COMPUTERS

OBJECTIVES Upon completion of this chapter, you will be able to:

1. Define the term "computer."
2. Explain the different classifications and types of computers.
3. Explain the different components of a computer system.
4. Explain the benefits and general applications of the computer.

Most drafters and drafting students have little or no background in the area of computers. The purpose of this chapter is to assist students in beginning to develop enough of a background in computers to allow for a study of the computer and its applications as a drafting tool.

Because of extraordinary technological developments during the past decade, the term "computer" is becoming a household word. Computer applications have expanded to such breadth and depth that the computer is now an integral part of the operations of virtually every type of business and industrial company. Very few occupations are practiced without at least indirect involvement with the computer.

Engineers and drafters have used computers for years in performing the mathematical operations that go with their jobs. However, an even more innovative computer application has begun to gain widespread acceptance: computer-aided drafting. Computer-aided drafting, or CAD as it is sometimes called, involves using the computer as a tool in making, checking, correcting, and revising original drawings. The computer can be used for converting a rough sketch into a finished working drawing, performing an infinite number of design computations, producing parts lists or bills of material, and many other drafting tasks.

The most important concept for students to understand in studying computer-aided drafting is that the computer is just the next phase in a long line of technological developments that have come about in an attempt to make the human drafter more efficient and more productive. The computer, by itself, does not make drawings. Drafters make drawings using the computer as a tool and, with the computer, they are able to make them faster, more neatly, and more accurately.

Before beginning a study of computer-aided drafting, students must first develop a basic understanding of computers in general. Drafting students should understand what a computer is, as well as what it is not, the classifications of computers, the types of computers, what software is, and the various components that make up a computer system.

HUMAN BEINGS VERSUS COMPUTERS

In many cases, a person's first experience with a computer is negative. Most people have been inconvenienced by a mistake that was blamed on a computer. An incorrect billing statement is issued, an airplane reservation is botched up, or an important shipment arrives late, and in each case the computer is blamed. Blaming the computer for what are really human errors has become common practice. However, it should be understood that computers are machines. They rarely make mistakes, but the people who operate them frequently do. An understanding of this concept is fundamental to developing an understanding of the computer.

A computer is an electronic machine that has storage, logic, and mathematical capabilities and has been designed to perform certain tasks at extremely fast speeds. The computer has four distinguishing characteristics: (1) Computers perform all operations electronically; (2) computers have an internal storage capability; (3) computers receive operational instructions from stored programs; and (4) computers can modify program executions by making logical decisions.

The computer has two capabilities that make it a particularly valuable tool for human use: (1) a computer is extraordinarily fast compared to human beings, and (2) a computer is much more accurate and reliable than a human being. On the other hand, the computer has two critical shortcomings. (1) A computer cannot reason and think as a human being can. Computers are capable of making decisions based on mathematical logic, but they cannot reason, apply common sense, make judgments, or use intuition. (2) A computer cannot adapt or innovate during the problem-solving process.

A computer that has been incorrectly programmed will simply keep plodding along making the same mistakes regardless of circumstances, until shut down and reprogrammed.

A computer is only capable of doing precisely what it is told and nothing more. This drawback can be illustrated by considering a sports contest between a computerized team and a human team. After carefully studying the other team and making special note of its weaknesses, the computerized team is programmed to play the game in a way designed to beat the other team. Shortly after the game begins, the computerized team begins to run up a commanding lead. Seeing this, the human team decides to innovate and try several new strategies. Because the computerized team was programmed to use certain plays, it simply continues to do so, but now with poor results. Because it was able to adapt and innovate during the game, the human team emerges victorious.

This example illustrates an important point about people and computers. People are well suited for thinking, reasoning, adapting, innovating, applying intuition, and learning from experience. Computers, on the other hand, are particularly suited for calculating, performing repetitive tasks, and making comparisons, all with a high degree of accuracy and reliability. This being the case, the computer can help people expand their capabilities considerably in certain areas if properly used. One of the newest, most innovative of these areas is drafting and design.

CLASSIFICATIONS OF COMPUTERS

Computers can be classified in a number of ways. The classification assigned a computer depends on the classification method being used. On one hand, computers may be classified according to the type of data they are capable of handling. When this is the classification method, computers are called either digital or analog. This is the most common classification method for grouping computers. On the other hand, computers may be classified according to the purpose they were designed to serve. When this is the case, they are classified as general-purpose or special-purpose computers. A final classification takes into account computers that combine a mixture of characteristics. Computers in this category are referred to as hybrid computers.

Analog Versus Digital Computers

The two main classifications of computers are digital and analog. The type familiar to most people is the digital computer because it is used in applications of high visibility and frequent human interaction. Most business and engineering computers, including those used in computer-aided drafting applications, are digital.

A *digital* computer receives input in the form of numbers, letters, or special characters. It converts these to electronic binary signals (Chapter 3) for processing and data manipulation. During the output stage, the binary signals are converted back into numbers, letters, and special characters that human beings can understand. Such things as lines, points, planes, curves, and various other geometric conditions used in drafting must be converted into binary form in order to input them. The process is known as *digitizing*. Data in the computer must be converted back into geometric forms by a plotter in order to make a drawing. This process is known as *plotting*. Both of these computer-aided drafting processes are discussed in depth in Chapters 5 and 6.

Analog computers do not operate on digits. Rather, they measure continuous physical magnitudes. Analog computers are often used to monitor and control the operation of machines and equipment. A computerized air-conditioning system for a large condominium complex might use an analog computer. The computer, in this case, would constantly measure temperature and humidity and cause the heating and cooling equipment to adjust to the current need. Other physical properties sometimes measured by analog computers are voltage, current, heat, light, pressure, and fluid flow.

Computer-aided drafters will use digital computers. They need not be concerned with analog computers except to know the differences between the two. Figures 1–1 through 1–3 present examples of commonly used digital computers.

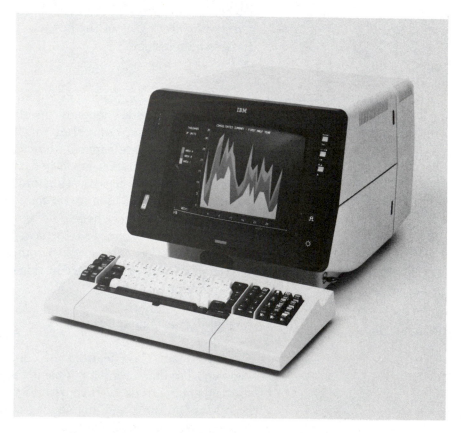

FIGURE 1–1 IBM 3279 Color Display Terminal. (Courtesy of IBM.)

FIGURE 1-2 Telex 276 Control Display Station. (Courtesy of Telex Computer Products, Inc.)

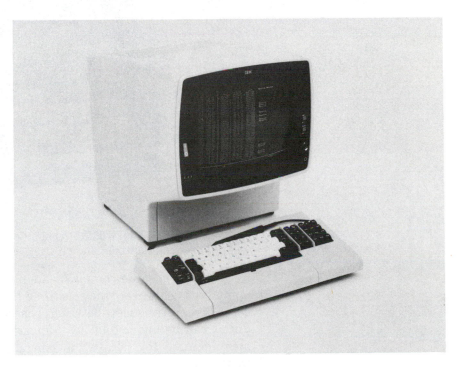

FIGURE 1-3 IBM 3278 Display Station. (Courtesy of IBM.)

General-Purpose, Special-Purpose, and Hybrid Computers

Computers can also be classified as being general purpose, special purpose, or hybrid. *General-purpose* computers, as the name implies, are designed to perform any number of different tasks. A home computer designed for sale to the general public is an example of a general-purpose computer. Computers designed to serve one limited, specific purpose are classified as *specific-purpose* computers. Some computers used in computer-aided drafting situations are special-purpose computers. In the simplest terms, *hybrid* computers are a cross between general- and special-purpose computers.

General-purpose computers have the advantage of flexibility. This allows for a much broader utilization of the computer, which can be an important factor in determining the cost effectiveness of purchasing a computer system. The primary disadvantage of a general-purpose computer is lack of speed. General-purpose computers are not able to perform tasks as quickly as special-purpose computers. Figures 1–4 through 1–6 present examples of general-purpose computers.

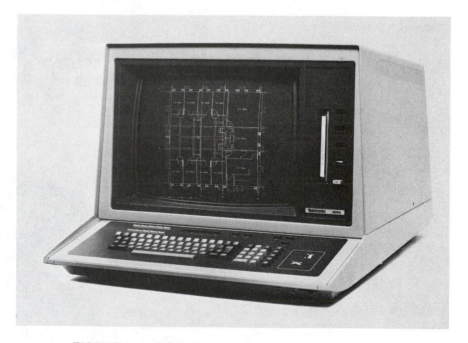

FIGURE 1–4 4054 Graphic Computing System. (Courtesy of Tektronix, Inc.)

Special-purpose computers are much faster than general-purpose computers. However, they sacrifice flexibility in gaining this advantage. The differences between general- and special-purpose computers can be understood by comparing an automobile designed and manufactured for sale to the general public with one especially designed for racing. The car sold to the general public will have a normal set of tires and several options for comfort and enjoyment, such as a plush interior, air conditioning, and a radio. Its engine and body

FIGURE 1-5 IBM 3033 Processor. (Courtesy of IBM.)

FIGURE 1-6 General-purpose computer. (Courtesy of AT&T Long Lines.)

will have been designed for general travel and transportation. The race car, on the other hand, is designed to win races. Therefore, it has been stripped of all luxuries, the engine has been modified, the body has been stripped away in some places and reinforced in others, and it has been given a special set of racing tires. The race car is a special-purpose car designed for one purpose, to win races. This it does quite well. However, in streamlining for speed, it has sacrificed flexibility. It can win races, but it cannot take the family on vacation, be driven to work, or be used for going to the store.

Hybrid computers combine the most desirable characteristics, speed and flexibility, of general- and special-purpose computers. The result is that they are able to perform tasks and solve problems much faster than a general-purpose computer while maintaining a high degree of flexibility and accuracy.

TYPES OF COMPUTERS

So far it has been learned that computers may be classified as to the types of data they can handle. When this is the case, they are classified as either digital or analog. It has also been learned that computers may be classified according to the purposes they will serve. When this is the case, they are classified as general-purpose, special-purpose, or hybrid computers.

The most common classification of computer is the digital computer. Computer-aided drafting systems make use of the digital computer. Consequently, this is the classification of computer with which the computer drafting technician should be the most familiar.

Although there are extremely large and complex "supercomputers," such as those used in the space program, most digital computers are either minicomputers or microcomputers.

Minicomputers

Until around the mid-1960s, the computer was an expensive, cumbersome machine. In spite of the size and cost problems, the computer was a valuable time- and work-saving device. Because of this, business and industry began to recognize numerous new applications for the computer. It was at this time that the need for a small, inexpensive, physically rugged computer was recognized. In response to this need, computer manufacturers developed the minicomputer.

Minicomputers achieved an almost immediate widescale acceptance and new applications multiplied. Business, education, industry, science, medicine, and the military were quick to recognize the value of the minicomputer. Its biggest advantage was that it was a full-scale computer with most of the capabilities of larger computers without the size and cost disadvantages.

The technological breakthrough that allowed for the development of the minicomputer was the integrated circuit (IC). Sometimes referred to as silicon chips, ICs are actually electronic circuits containing many conventional components (i.e., resistors, capacitors, transistors) that are assembled on a chip of silicon that may be smaller than a child's fingernail (Figure 1-7). Hundreds of silicon chips may be mounted on a single printed circuit board. In this way, a computer, which at one time would fill an entire room, can be reduced to a minicomputer no larger than a small television set. Figures 1-8 and 1-9 present examples of minicomputers.

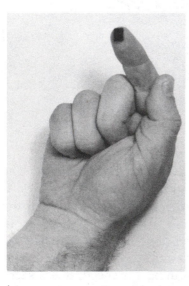

FIGURE 1-7 Modern IC chip.

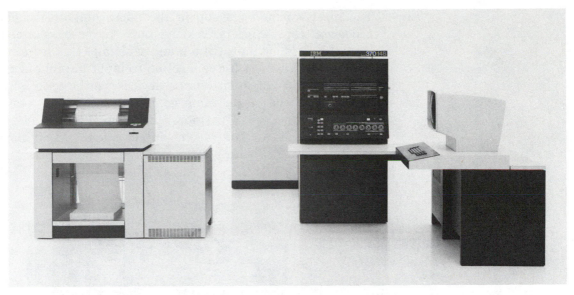

FIGURE 1-8 IBM 370/148 Design Model. (Courtesy of IBM.)

FIGURE 1-9 IBM 3033 Processor and 370 Design Model. (Courtesy of IBM.)

Microcomputers

A microcomputer is a computer that is manufactured on a single printed circuit board that contains one or more chips. Microcomputers are the result of technological advances that allow over 100,000 electronic components to be contained in a single chip.

The most common makeup of the microcomputer is: (1) a microprocessor chip which serves the same purpose as a conventional central processing unit, (2) a number of chips that serve as the memory, and (3) circuitry for connection to input/output devices.

A number of input/output devices can be used with a microcomputer. Some of the more commonly used are typewriters, line printers, magnetic cassette tapes, and floppy disks. A microcomputer commonly used by the general public is the TRS-80 manufactured by Radio Shack (Figure 1-10).

FIGURE 1-10 TRS-80 Model II Microcomputer. (Courtesy of Radio Shack, a Division of Tandy Corporation.)

COMPUTER SYSTEM COMPONENTS

The term "computer" is commonly used in referring to what would better be described as a computer system. Problems are solved and tasks are performed by people interacting with computer systems, not just the computer.

A complete computer system consists of various articles of hardware and software. The central processing unit (CPU), cathode ray terminal (CRT), printer, hard-copy unit, and numerous other input/output and auxiliary storage devices are all classified as *hardware*. Programs, flowcharts, and various other forms of documentation are classified as *software*. Hardware and software together make up a computer system.

The Central Processing Unit

The central processing unit (CPU) of a computer system controls all functions of the system. In fact, the CPU is the computer. All other hardware items are peripheral equipment for input, output, and external storage. The CPU contains two separate components: the control section and the logic or arithmetic section (Figure 1-11).

The control section of a CPU actually directs the computer system in all operations. Its functions include entering data into storage, calling data up from storage, executing programmed instructions, relaying information between storage and input/output devices, and controlling the logic section.

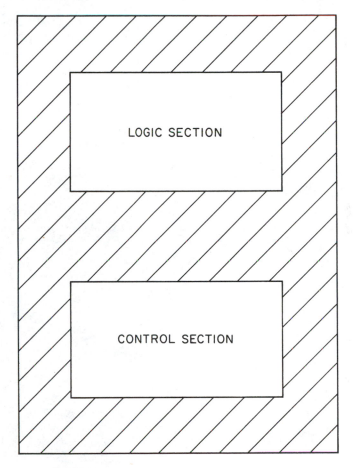

FIGURE 1-11   Component parts of the CPU.

The logic section actually performs all computer operations, such as math functions, decision making, comparing, sorting, selecting, editing, and converting of data. The relationship of the two components of the CPU can be understood by considering the relationship of a car and its driver. The driver or control section directs all of the car's operations. However, it is the car or logic section which actually performs all operations, such as turning, stopping, moving forward, and moving in reverse. Figures 1-12 and 1-13 present examples of CPUs.

FIGURE 1-12 IBM 3380 Direct Access Storage Model. (Courtesy of IBM.)

FIGURE 1-13 IBM 370/148 (close-up). (Courtesy of IBM.)

Input/Output Devices

Using a computer involves three steps: inputting of data, processing of data, and outputting of data (Figure 1-14). Inputting and out-putting of data are accomplished by various special devices designed for these purposes. Some devices may be used strictly for input and some strictly for output, whereas others can be used for both input and output.

In order to solve a problem or perform a task, a computer must have programmed instructions and accompanying data. These things are entered into the computer via an input device. After processing,

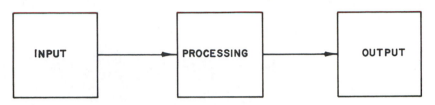

FIGURE 1-14   Steps in operating a computer.

data are converted into a form usable by human beings by output devices. Commonly used input/output devices include CRT terminals, card readers, keyboards, and magnetic disks, drums, or tapes. Figures 1-15 through 1-20 present examples of some commonly used input/output devices.

FIGURE 1-15   Telex 276/278 Controller and Display Station. (Courtesy of Telex Computer Products, Inc.)

FIGURE 1-16   Input/output device. (Courtesy of AT&T Long Lines.)

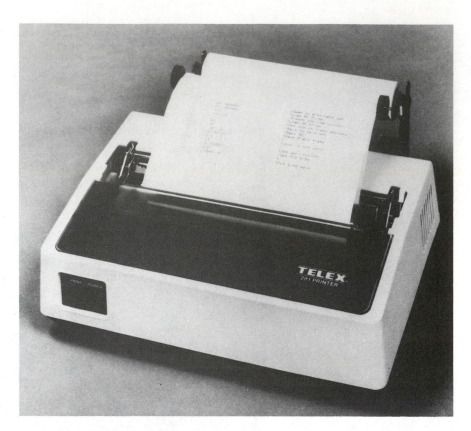

FIGURE 1-17 Telex 281 Printer. (Courtesy of Telex Computer Products, Inc.)

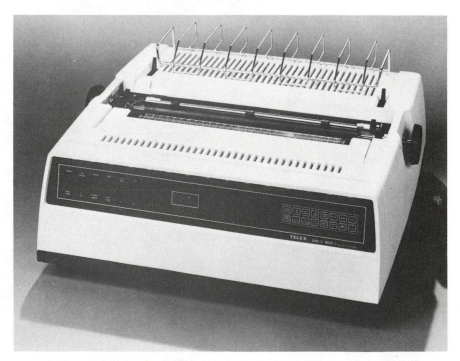

FIGURE 1-18 Telex 286C MOD 1 Printer Terminal. (Courtesy of Telex Computer Products, Inc.)

FIGURE 1-19   IBM 3525 Card Punch. (Courtesy of IBM.)

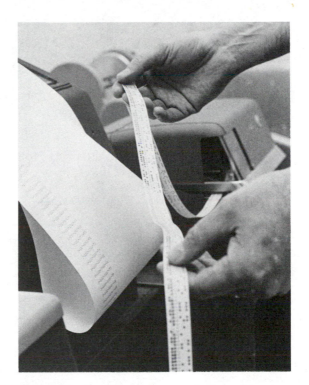

FIGURE 1-20   Auxiliary storage device. (Courtesy of AT&T Long Lines.)

Auxiliary Storage Devices

Computers are often rated according to speed of performance and storage capacity. It is often necessary to increase the storage capacity of a computer. This can be accomplished by adding auxiliary storage devices.

These devices are specialized pieces of equipment designed to handle various types of auxiliary storage media, such as magnetic tapes, disks, paper tapes, and various other forms of storage media. Figures 1-21 through 1-25 present examples of auxiliary storage devices.

FIGURE 1-21 IBM 3420 Magnetic Tape Unit. (Courtesy of IBM.)

FIGURE 1-22 Auxiliary storage device. (Courtesy of AT&T Long Lines.)

FIGURE 1-23 Auxiliary storage device. (Courtesy of AT&T Long Lines.)

FIGURE 1-24 Telex Series 80 Magnetic Tape Sub-System. (Courtesy of Telex Computer Products, Inc.)

FIGURE 1-25 TRS-80 Model II Disk System. (Courtesy of Radio Shack, a Division of Tandy Corporation.)

Software and User Programs

The key to the flexibility of any computer system is its software. This concept can be understood by drawing a correlation between a computer system and a race car. Regardless of how well designed and outfitted a race car is, it will only perform as well as the driver who takes it through the paces. In this analogy, the race car is the hardware and the driver is the software.

Computer systems operate on instructions received through programs and data provided by users through some type of input device. These programs and various other operating aids are known as software. Programs for guiding the computer through general operations such as transferring data to an output medium are referred to as *utility programs* or sometimes as *firmware*. Utility programs are usually supplied by the computer manufacturer. If the computer is a general-purpose computer, utility programs may be provided in the form of diskettes or tapes. If the computer is a special-purpose computer, utility programs may be designed into the hardware. It is in this case that the programs are sometimes referred to as firmware.

Programs that direct the computer to perform very specific or highly specialized tasks for a particular application are known as *user programs*. User programs may be developed by the user company, by software companies, or by individuals on a freelance basis. Another source of user programs available to companies that purchase certain computer systems is the user's library.

The user's library is a collection of user programs that have been developed by companies or individuals who use a particular computer system. These programs are cataloged by computer manufacturers and made available at reduced prices, on a rental basis, or through library loan to users of their computer system (Figure 1–26).

COMPUTER BENEFITS AND APPLICATIONS

The list of benefits afforded business, industry, education, government, and the medical world by computers is extensive already and growing daily. There seems to be no end to the ever-expanding capabilities of the human–computer team.

Human beings and computers complement each other perfectly. A computer cannot think, reason, or innovate; but human beings can. People are not very fast, accurate, or reliable; but computers are. Taken together, human beings and computers can make up a team with extraordinary capabilities, the limits of which we have not even begun to approach.

The computer's speed, accuracy, and storage-recall capabilities make its potential for constantly increasing applications almost limitless. The list of computer applications is already impressive. The computer is used as a management tool for forecasting, planning, cost estimation, inventory, budgeting, scheduling, and evaluation. It is used as an educational tool for individualizing instruction, test scoring, record keeping, grade reporting, and research.

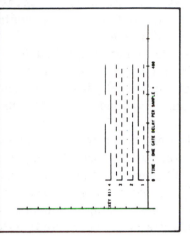

ABSTRACT #: 51/00-1403/0

Title: Analysis of Logic Circuit Behavior

Author: K.J. Orford
Physics Department
Durham University
South Road, Durham, England

Memory Requirement: 16K
Statements: 325
Files: 1 ASCII Program

This program stores the interrelationships of logic elements (gates, latches, etc.) in a complex circuit, and predicts the state of all the elements a short time later. The program then has three optional modes. It can stop and print out, or continue and predict the next state and print until stopped, or continually predict subsequent states and show a selected number (up to 12) as waveform on the display. The three modes are selected by User-Definable Keys. Up to eight input lines may be used and changed at will during execution by pressing the User-Definable Keys.

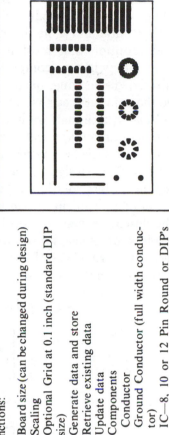

ABSTRACT #: 51/00-1404/0

Title: Circuitboard Patterns

Author: Jan Beckman
Imperial Oil Ltd.
Edmonton, Alberta, Canada

Memory Requirements: 16K
Peripherals: 4051R05 Binary ROM Pack
4952 Joystick
4662 Plotter

Statements: 496
Files: 1 ASCII Program
2 ASCII Data (one is example)
2 Binary Program
1 Scratch (for example)
(First 6 on tape or reassign File # variables)

You can draw circuitboard patterns on the 4050 screen with this program. Once you are satisfied with the pattern, draw it on the 4662 Plotter. Use a Mylar pen in the Plotter and draw your foil pattern on a copper board right on the Plotter. The Mylar pen works as an etch-resist pencil would.

Functions:

Board size (can be changed during design)
Scaling
Optional Grid at 0.1 inch (standard DIP size)
Generate data and store
Retrieve existing data
Update data
Components
Conductor
Ground Conductor (full width conductor)
IC—8, 10 or 12 Pin Round or DIP's (horizontal or vertical) or other pin numbers specifying your own width
Solderpad
Resistor Pads
Edge Connector Strip
Transistor Pads
Move without drawing
End (closes all files)

Test data is included to familiarize yourself with the program. Note precautions on program MARKing data files automatically.

FIGURE 1-26 Page from Tektronix "User's Library." (Courtesy of Tektronix, Inc.)

19

The computer is used as an administrative tool for accounting purposes, payroll, budgeting, benefits computations, and record keeping. It is used increasingly in manufacturing for drawings verification, numerical control of machines, cost estimation versus actual cost comparisons, stock inventory and control, quality control, product testing, and product shipping and billing.

Computer usage in the medical world has attained such widespread adoption that most hospitals and laboratories simply could not operate without computers. Patient records, insurance claims, admitting, discharging, diagnosis, monitoring, and medication all involve the computer as a vital tool.

Finally, although we have really only begun to scratch the surface of computer applications, the computer is used by engineers, designers, architects, and drafters in all phases of the design process (Figure 1-27). Design is the process of combining scientific principles, new ideas, old ideas, and sometimes existing products to the solution of a problem or the meeting of a need. There are five steps in the design process: (1) problem identification; (2) formulation of new ideas or concepts; (3) proposed solutions; (4) models, prototypes, or trial runs; and (5) working drawings.

The computer is used in the problem identification stage to col-

FIGURE 1-27 The design process.

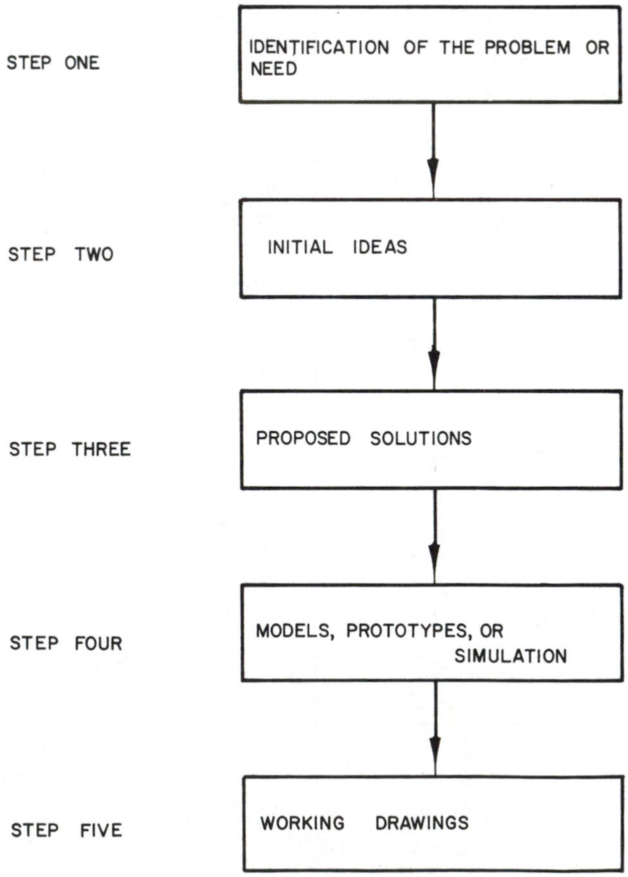

lect, store, and call up raw data which can be used in limiting the problem. It is used in the new-ideas stage for recording thoughts and calling up old concepts that might spawn new ideas. The computer is used in the proposed-solutions stage for comparing possible solutions and helping designers arrive at compromises that are based on all available information.

The final two stages of the design process are where the computer is being used most innovatively. In the trial-run stage, designers, in the past, have been shackled by the need for constructing time-consuming models or prototypes so that proposed design solutions could be tested under actual conditions. Through simulation, the computer has substantially reduced the need for expensive models and prototypes. A new design and the desired conditions may now be placed in the computer, displayed on the CRT screen, and observed by the designer (Figures 1-28 and 1-29).

In the final or working-drawing stage of the design process, drafters are provided with the raw data needed to develop working drawings so that production can begin. In times past, this has meant using a drafting board, drafting machine, and various drafting instruments to convert sketches or models into completed working drawings. Often, it now means using a modern computer drafting system (Figure 1-30).

FIGURE 1-28   4014-1 Computer Display Terminal. (Courtesy of Tektronix, Inc.)

FIGURE 1-29 Computer terminal for office planning. (Courtesy of AT&T Long Lines.)

FIGURE 1-30 AD 380 Computer-Aided Drafting System. (Courtesy of Auto-trol Technology Corporation.)

SUMMARY AND REVIEW

- Engineers and drafters have used computers for years in performing mathematical computations. Now an even more innovative computer application is emerging: computer-aided drafting.

- The most important concept to understand about computer-aided drafting is that the computer, by itself, does not make drawings. Drafters make drawings using the computer as a tool.

- A computer can be defined as an electronic machine which has storage, logic, and mathematical capabilities and can perform tasks at extremely fast speeds.

- The computer has four distinguishing characteristics: (1) performs all operations electronically; (2) has an internal storage capability; (3) receives operational instructions from stored programs; and (4) can modify program executions by making logical decisions.

- The computer has two capabilities that make it a particularly valuable tool for human use: (1) extraordinarily fast; and (2) extremely accurate and reliable.

- A computer has two critical shortcomings: (1) cannot think, reason, or innovate; and (2) cannot adapt during the problem-solving process.

- When computers are classified according to the type of data they are capable of handling, they are classified as being either digital or analog.

- When computers are classified according to the purpose they serve, they are classified as general purpose or special purpose.

- A special classification given to computers that combine a mixture of characteristics is the hybrid classification.

- The most commonly used type of computer is the digital computer.

- General-purpose computers have the advantage of flexibility, which allows for broader utilization, but sacrifices speed.

- Special-purpose computers are very fast, but they sacrifice flexibility.

- The most common types of digital computers are the minicomputer and the microcomputer.

- Minicomputers have most of the capabilities of full-scale computers without the size and cost disadvantages.

- The technological breakthrough that allowed for the development of minicomputers was the integrated circuit (IC).

- A microcomputer is a computer that is manufactured on a single printed circuit board which contains one or more IC chips.

- Most microcomputers have three components: (1) a microprocessor chip which serves as the CPU; (2) a number of chips to serve as memory; and (3) circuitry for connection to input/output devices.

- A complete computer system is made up of several different components, which include the CPU, input/output devices, auxiliary storage devices, and software and user programs.

- Taken together a computer and a human being can make a very capable team because their strengths complement one another and their weaknesses offset each other's.

- The list of computer applications is extensive and getting longer daily. Industry, business, education, medicine, government, and the military have already found hundreds of applications for the computer.

SELF-TEST Directions

This self-test is provided to allow you to test your retention and understanding of the subject matter covered in this chapter. Respond to all questions without referring back to the chapter. After completing the self-test, refer to the chapter text and check your answers. Reread the material covering any question that you miss before proceeding to the next chapter.

1. Indicate whether each of the following statements is true or false.
   a. Together human beings and computers can make up a very capable team because their strengths are complementary while their weaknesses are offsetting.
   b. Minicomputers are smaller and less costly than full-scale computers, but they do not have nearly the capabilities.
   c. The most commonly used type of computer is the analog computer.
   d. Engineers and drafters have used computers for years in performing mathematical operations.
   e. The list of computer applications has grown rapidly over the past decade, but it has now reached its peak.

2. What is the most important concept to understand about computer-aided drafting?

3. Define the term "computer."

4. Explain the advantages and disadvantages of general-purpose computers.

5. Explain the advantages and disadvantages of special-purpose computers.

6. Define the term "microcomputer."

7. What was the technological breakthrough that allowed for the development of minicomputers?

8. A special classification of computers that combine various characteristics is the:
   a. Digital computer
   b. Analog computer
   c. Special-purpose computer
   d. General-purpose computer
   e. Hybrid computers
   f. Microcomputer

9. When computers are classified according to the purpose they will serve, they are classified as:
   a. Digital computers
   b. Analog computers
   c. Special-purpose computers
   d. General-purpose computers
   e. Hybrid computer
   f. Microcomputers

10. When computers are classified according to the type of data they are capable of handling, they are classified as:
    a. Digital computers
    b. Analog computers
    c. Special-purpose computers
    d. General-purpose computers
    e. Hybrid computers
    f. Microcomputers

11. A computer has two critical shortcomings. Which of the following are they?
    a. Cannot think or reason
    b. Unreliable and inaccurate
    c. Unable to perform long, arduous tasks
    d. Cannot adapt or innovate during problem solving

12. What are the two most common types of digital computers?

13. Most microcomputers have three components. Name them.

14. Name four components of a complete computer system.

15. What are the four distinguishing characteristics of the computer?

16. The computer has two capabilities that make it a particularly valuable tool for human use. What are they?

2

COMMUNICATING WITH COMPUTERS

OBJECTIVES   Upon completion of this chapter, you will be able to:

1. Explain the problem-solving steps.
2. Demonstrate an understanding of simple program and systems flowcharting techniques.
3. Demonstrate an understanding of BASIC language programming.

The computer is an amazing electronic machine that has allowed human beings to expand their problem-solving capabilities substantially in a number of fields, one of them being drafting. Computers represent what is probably the most significant technological breakthrough since the Industrial Revolution. However, like all machines, computers can only do what human beings make them do.

In order to solve a problem or perform a task, the computer must be programmed to do so. A program is a complete set of instructions which tell the computer exactly what to do. One important characteristic of a program is that it must be written in a language that the computer can understand. People who are especially trained to write computer programs are called *computer programmers*.

Computer programmers take instructions which have been written in human terms and convert them to the appropriate computer language so that the computer can understand them. It is not necessary for a computer drafting technician to be a computer programmer. Although there are some computer drafting technicians who become quite skilled in computer programming, most consider themselves computer-aided drafting system operators and leave the programming to the programmers.

On the other hand, however, computer programmers are not drafters. Consequently, they do not have the knowledge of drafting necessary to write programs that will make computers perform drafting tasks. This knowledge gap between programming and drafting has been the primary inhibitor of the development of computer-aided drafting software. The problem is being resolved by close interaction and communication between drafting and programming personnel. This interaction has now produced some highly sophisticated, effective software which has, in turn, made wide-scale adoption of computer-aided drafting a reality.

A computer drafting technician does not have to be a highly skilled computer programmer. Computer programming is a separate career field unto itself and requires as much highly technical training as drafting. However, computer drafting technicians should be able to communicate with programmers so that, together, they can develop the software necessary to make the computer a functional drafting tool. This is important because software is the key to the capability of a computer in a drafting setting or any other application.

In order to contribute to the development of usable software, computer drafting technicians must be familiar with how software is developed. This means becoming familiar with the computer programming steps, systems flowcharting, program flowcharting, and a commonly used computer programming language.

The reason for becoming familiar with a computer programming language is so that computer drafting technicians can understand how programmers must go about communicating with computers. The most common problem-solving computer languages are FORTRAN, COBOL, and BASIC. Some CAD systems are designed to speak one of these commonly used computer languages. Others are designed to speak a variation of one of the commonly used languages, and others use a language that has been developed especially for that system. Regardless of the language used in a CAD system, if drafters are familiar with the programming steps, simple systems flowcharting, simple program flowcharting, and one of the commonly used programming languages, they will be able to communicate with programmers well enough to help develop effective CAD software. The purpose of this chapter is to give students an overview of the methods used in developing software for communicating with computers.

COMPUTER PROGRAMMING STEPS

Before a computer can perform a desired task, it must be programmed to do so. Before writing a computer program, a programmer must do three things: (1) develop a thorough understanding of the task to determine if it can be feasibly performed by the computer (the computer is not always the best answer); (2) determine the capabilities of the computer system which will be used to perform the task; and (3) determine exactly what the end product or output is supposed to be (a drawing, printout, letter, inventory list, etc.).

Once a programmer determines that a task can be performed on the computer system that is available, and that the system can provide the desired output, the development of a program which will make the computer perform the desired task can begin. The steps used in writing a program are problem analysis, determination of the method of solution, flowcharting, coding, translation, debugging, and documentation (Figure 2-1).

Problem analysis involves gathering all pertinent data related to the problem and making a determination as to whether the problem can be solved on the computer. The terms "problem" and "task" may be used interchangeably, but *problem* is the more commonly used term. Determining a method of solution means developing a step-by-step plan for solving the problem.

Flowcharting involves developing a symbolic illustration of all the logic and steps involved in solving the problem. Making a flowchart in programming is the equivalent of showing all the steps used

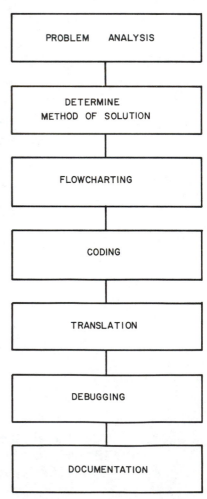

FIGURE 2-1 Computer programming steps.

in solving a math problem. Just as some students can solve a problem without writing down all the steps, some programmers can develop programs without making a flowchart. However, this practice is not encouraged because it can lead to problems later.

The *coding* step involves actually writing a program in the appropriate computer language. In the *translation* step, the computer translates the program into binary signals, which is all that the computer really understands. *Debugging* means trying the program out on a trial basis and working out any snags. *Documentation* is a complete running narrative explaining everything that was done in developing the program, problems that were incurred, how the problems were overcome, and any other information that the programmer deems pertinent. Program documentation also includes a flowchart and a listing of the program. The most important of these steps for the drafter to understand are flowcharting and coding.

OVERVIEW OF FLOWCHARTING

This section presents an overview of flowcharting. There are two types of flowcharts: systems flowcharts and program flowcharts. A *systems* flowchart shows the flow of data through a system and the sequence of operations that take place within a system (Figure 2-2).

FIGURE 2-2 Sample systems flowchart.

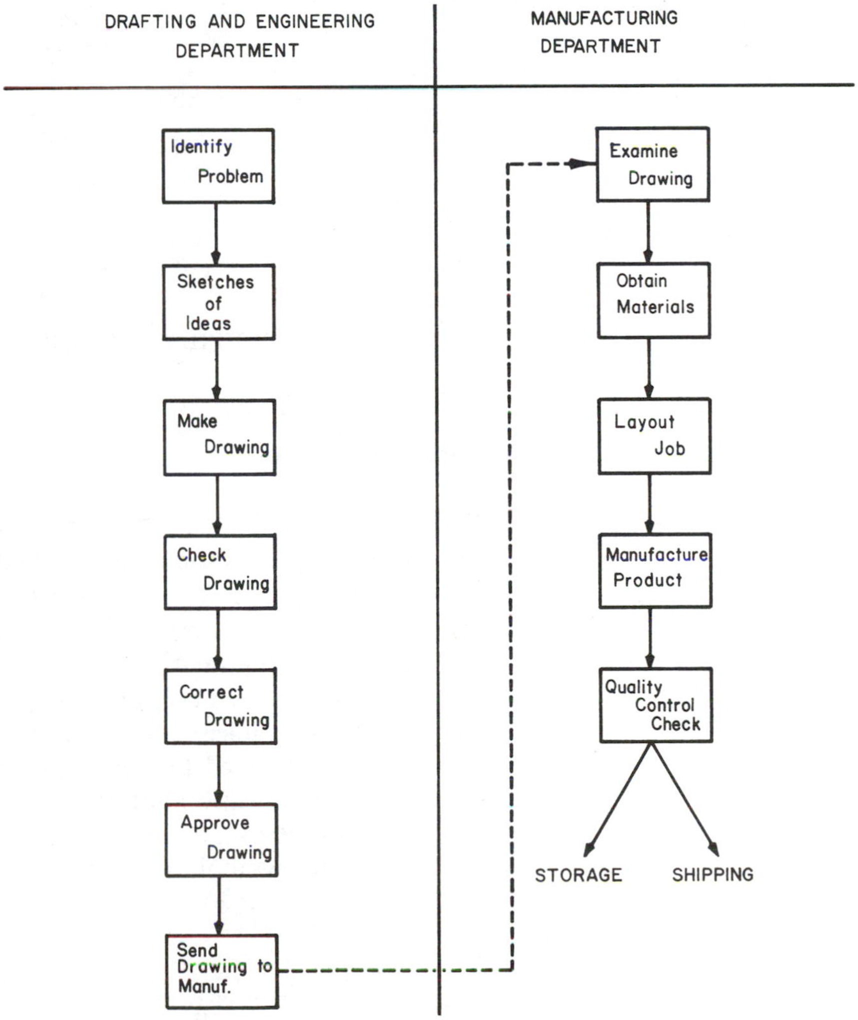

A *program* flowchart is a pictorial representation of the detailed steps in solving a problem (Figure 2-3). One operation shown in a systems flowchart, if it involves the computer, might require several program flowcharts to complete it. Program flowcharting relates more directly to the job of the computer drafting technician. However, the drafter should also be familiar with systems flowcharting.

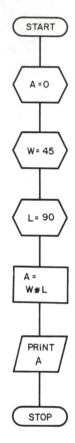

FIGURE 2-3   Sample program flowchart.

Systems Flowcharting

Systems flowcharts can be used to show the interrelationships of operations and the various departments in which they take place or to show the operations performed to produce a certain output. Systems flowcharts are comprised of symbols and lines.

The most frequently used systems flowcharting symbols are the input/output symbol, process symbol, flowline symbol, annotation symbol, connector symbol, punched card symbol, magnetic tape symbol, punched tape symbol, document symbol, manual input symbol, communication link symbol, display symbol, card deck symbol, card file symbol, on-line storage symbol, off-line storage symbol, magnetic disk symbol, magnetic drum symbol, core storage symbol, auxiliary operation symbol, manual operation symbol, extract symbol, sort symbol, and collate symbol. Figure 2-4 presents the systems flowcharting symbols recommended by the American National Standards Institute (ANSI).

Systems flowcharts are prepared in such a way that processing

FIGURE 2-4 Systems flowchart symbols.

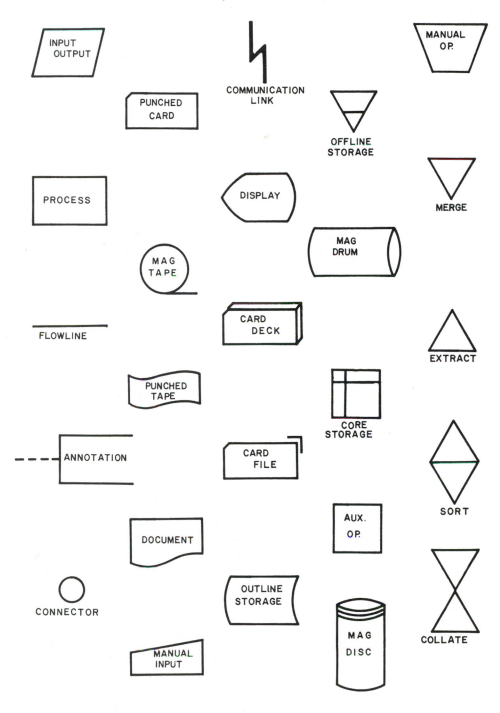

steps are read from top to bottom and left to right (Figure 2–5). A systems flowchart can be a valuable aid in that it gives an easy-to-understand picture of relationships that would otherwise be difficult to explain. Systems flowcharts are usually done by systems analysts. Once completed, programmers may then be called on to develop program flowcharts for carrying out computer operations that may be required.

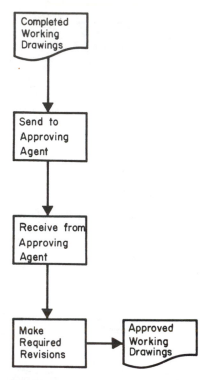

FIGURE 2–5   Flowcharts use top-to-bottom and left-to-right orientation.

Program Flowcharting

A program flowchart is a pictorial representation of the steps necessary to solve a problem or perform a task (Figure 2–6). The purpose of a program flowchart is to provide a symbolic representation of the processes the computer must perform in solving a problem.

Program flowcharts are sometimes referred to as *logic diagrams* because they illustrate the logic of a computer program. They are prepared before computer programs are written and can be valuable aids to the programmer.

A program flowchart might be used in a number of different ways. It could be used as the starting point in writing a program, as a reference in working out the "bugs" in a program, or as documentation of a program. Figure 2–7 presents a flowchart that illustrates the steps involved in performing an everyday domestic chore: going to the store to buy a carton of milk.

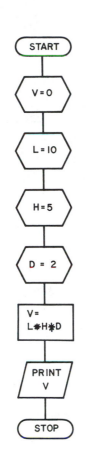

FIGURE 2-6   Sample program flowchart.

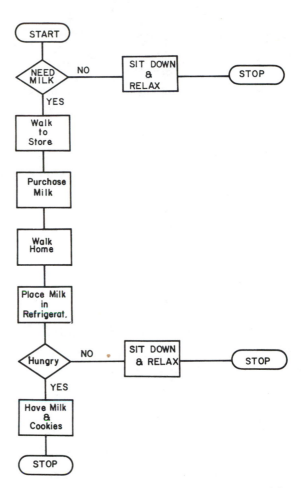

FIGURE 2-7   Flowchart of the steps one might go through in going to the store for a carton of milk.

Program flowcharting symbols

Program flowcharts consist of a series of single lines and symbols. A knowledge of these symbols is fundamental to an understanding of program flowcharting. The most frequently used program flowcharting symbols are the input/output symbol, process symbol, flowline symbol, annotation symbol, connector symbol, terminal/interrupt symbol, decision symbol, and preparation symbol. Figure 2-8 presents the program flowcharting symbols recommended by the American National Standards Institute (ANSI).

The *input/output* symbol is used to indicate any input or output function. The function might be "read," "print," "plot," or any other input/output function. A descriptor of the specific function is written inside the input/output symbol (Figure 2-9).

The *process* symbol is used to indicate any processing that must occur during execution of a program. The process might be add, subtract, multiply, divide, or any one of many other processes. A descriptor of the specific process is written inside the process symbol (Figure 2-10).

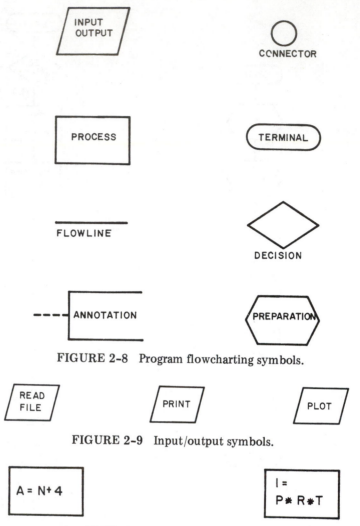

FIGURE 2-8   Program flowcharting symbols.

FIGURE 2-9   Input/output symbols.

FIGURE 2-10   Process symbols.

The *flowline* symbol is used to connect all other symbols. Flowcharts are normally read from top to bottom and left to right. When this rule is followed, the flowline symbol, by itself, is sufficient. If the flow deviates from the normal top-to-bottom, left-to-right mode, arrowheads must be added to indicate direction (Figure 2-11).

The *annotation* symbol is used when a comment, reminder, or clarification must be added to a flowchart. The annotation symbol does not indicate a decision, process, input, output, or any other action within a program. It is merely a means by which the programmer can attach a reminder, comment, or clarification to a flowchart for future reference (Figure 2-12).

The *connector* symbol is used a great deal in long or complicated flowcharts. There are two different types of connectors: on-page connectors and off-page connectors. *On-page* connectors indicate an exit from one part of a flowchart and entry to another part of the flowchart on the same page (Figure 2-13). *Off-page* connectors are used when a flowchart requires more than one page. Page references are used together with off-page connectors for clarity (Figure 2-14).

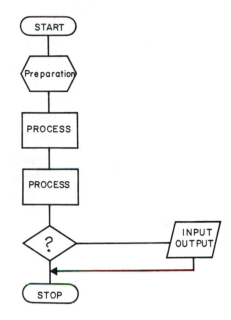

FIGURE 2-11   Arrowheads are used to indicate a change from the normal flow.

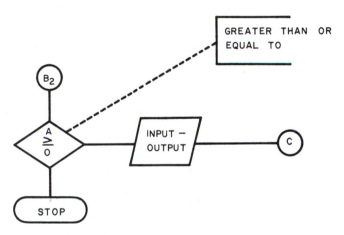

FIGURE 2-12   Annotation symbol.

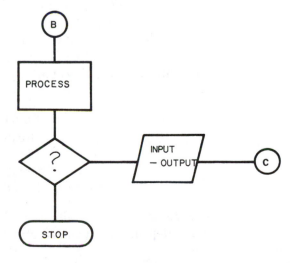

FIGURE 2-13   On-page connectors.

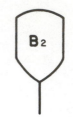

FIGURE 2-14   Off-page connectors.

The *terminal or interrupt* symbol is the most frequently used symbol because it comes at the beginning and the end of all flowcharts. It can also be used to indicate a break in the direction of flow. A terminal symbol used at the beginning of a flowchart contains the word "start." A terminal symbol used at the conclusion of a flowchart contains the word "end" or "stop." (Figure 2-15).

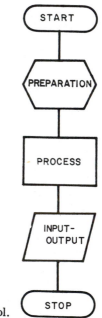

FIGURE 2-15   Terminal symbol.

The *decision* symbol is used when a decision must be made in a program. Program decisions are usually mathematical comparisons, such as "equal to," "greater than," "less than," "less than or equal to," and "greater than or equal to." These types of comparisons are indicated in a flowchart by using the following common math symbols:

$$= \quad \text{Equal to}$$
$$> \quad \text{Greater than}$$
$$< \quad \text{Less than}$$
$$>= \text{ or } \geq \quad \text{Greater than or equal to}$$
$$<= \text{ or } \leq \quad \text{Less than or equal to}$$

The decision symbol allows the program to take one of two directions, depending on the result of the comparison. A "yes" decision will branch off to some specified action, whereas a "no" will fall through to some other action (Figure 2-16).

The *preparation* symbol is used to get the program ready for the operations it will perform. It is used for control, initialization, and overhead. Preparation symbols are placed in a flowchart immediately after the start symbol (Figure 2-17). Figures 2-18 and 2-19 contain examples of completed flowcharts.

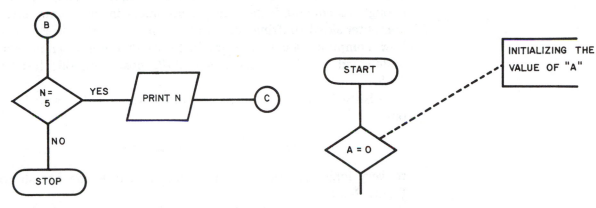

FIGURE 2-16   Decision symbol.   FIGURE 2-17   Preparation symbol.

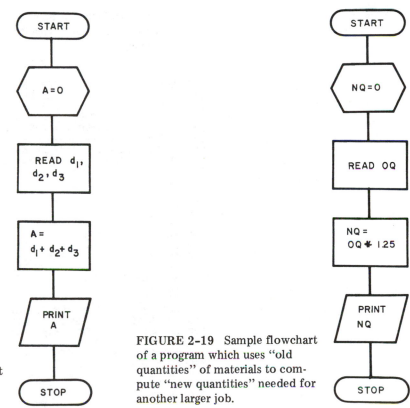

FIGURE 2-18   Sample flowchart of a program which adds dimensions.

FIGURE 2-19   Sample flowchart of a program which uses "old quantities" of materials to compute "new quantities" needed for another larger job.

OVERVIEW OF BASIC LANGUAGE PROGRAMMING

In order to be used as a problem-solving tool, the computer must be given a program for instructions and a set of data to operate on. Programs are operated by computer programmers and data are provided by computer users. The trend is toward easier-to-use software that can be developed and used by nonprogrammers. However, at present, writing computer programs is a highly technical skill that requires in-depth, specialized training.

If drafters are familiar with one computer language, they will be able to understand how the various computer languages work well enough to communicate with programmers in developing effective computer-aided drafting software. The language that best illustrates how computer languages work in terms that nonprogrammers can understand is BASIC (Beginner's All-Purpose Symbolic Instruction Code).

BASIC programs can range from simple one-liners such as this one

```
10 PRINT "THIS IS A BASIC PROGRAM"
```

to very long and complicated programs such as the one shown in Figure 2-20.

Learning to use BASIC involves learning several BASIC statements. The most frequently used BASIC statements are LET, IF, PRINT, GOTO, READ, DATA, REM, and END. In the following paragraphs, each of these statements is presented individually.

FIGURE 2-20 Sample of a long program. (Courtesy of Earl N. Gulledge, Vice-President, Okaloosa-Walton Junior College.)

```
                         SAMPLE PROGRAM

100 REM PROGRAM BY DR. EARL N. GULLEDGE
110 REM PROGRAM CALCULATES MEAN, VARIANCE, AND STANDARD DEVIATION
120 CLS
130 PRINT "ENTER THE X VARIABLE AND DEPRESS"
140 PRINT "THE ENTER KEY AFTER EACH ENTRY"
150 PRINT "--------------------------------"
160 PRINT "WHEN YOU HAVE ENTERED ALL ENTRIES"
170 PRINT "ENTER ZERO (0) AND PRESS ENTER"
180 LET N = 0
190 LET X1 = 0
200 LET X2 = 0
210 PRINT
220 INPUT X
230 PRINT
240 IF X = 0 GOTO 300
250 LET N = N + 1 : REM TOTALS NUMBER OF ENTRIES
260 LET X1 = X1 + X : REM TOTALS SUM OF ENTRIES
270 LET X2 = X2 + X↑2 : REM X↑2 = X SQUARED : REM TOTALS SUM OF
    ENTRIES SQUARED
280 LET X = 0
290 GOTO 220
300 LET X3 = X1/N   : REM COMPUTES MEAN
310 REM LINE 320 COMPUTES VARIANCE
320 LET S1 = (N * X2 - X1↑2)/N↑2 : REM X1↑2 = X1 SQUARED,
    N↑2 = N SQUARED
330 REM LINE 340 COMPUTES STANDARD DEVIATION
340 SD = SQR(S1)
350 PRINT "              SUM OF RESPONSES = ";X1
360 PRINT "              SUM OF RESPONSES SQUARED = ";X2
370 PRINT "              TOTAL NUMBER OF RESPONSES = ";N
380 PRINT "              MEAN OF RESPONSES = ";X3
390 PRINT "              STANDARD DEVIATION = ";SD
400 PRINT "              VARIANCE = ";S1
410 PRINT
```

The LET Statement

The following example is a portion of a BASIC program using the LET statement:

```
10  LET A = 5
20  LET B = 6
30  LET C = 7
40  LET D = A + B + C
```

Notice that in a BASIC program each line begins with a number and that the numbers increase in multiples greater than 1. In the case of the example above, the first line was numbered 10 and all lines thereafter increased by increments of 10. Actually, any numbers could have been used. However, the numbers 10 or 100 or the most commonly used starting points in BASIC programs and 10 is the most frequently used increment. An increment is used to allow the programmer to insert new lines between lines without having to start over or renumber.

The LET statement, as can be seen from the example, is used to assign a value to a variable or to assign the result of a calculation to a variable. In the sample above, the computer has in storage several values, which have been named A(5), B(6), and C(7). It has also reserved a storage space for the variable D. Before the program is executed, which will result in the addition of the stored values for A, B, and C, the computer's storage locations appear as shown in Figure 2-21. When the program is executed, the zero in the D storage location will be replaced by the value 18 (A + B + C).

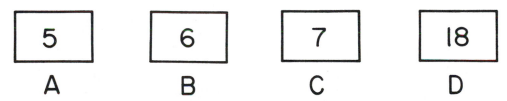

FIGURE 2-21 Computer storage locations.

In BASIC, memory locations may be designated by single characters from the alphabet such as A, B, C, . . . , X, Y, or Z. They may also be designated by single letters of the alphabet followed by single numerical digits, such as X1, C3, D2, F4, T7. These are the only acceptable ways of designating variables (and hence storage locations) in BASIC.

The IF Statement

The IF statement allows decisions to be built into a program. BASIC decisions are of an "if this, then that" nature. IF decisions include the following mathematical comparisons:

    = Equals
    > Greater than

$<$ Less than
$>=$ or $\geqslant$ Greater than or equal to
$<=$ or $\leqslant$ Less than or equal to
$<>$ Not equal

IF statements increase the flexibility of a BASIC program. The following program contains examples of IF statements:

```
10  LET B = 15
20  IF A = B THEN 50
30  IF A > B THEN 60
35  PRINT "A IS LESS THAN 15"
40  STOP
50  PRINT "A EQUALS 15"
55  STOP
60  PRINT "A IS GREATER THAN 15"
```

In line 10, the value for B has been set at 15. In line 20, the value that is input for A is tested against B. If A = B (if they are both 15), the computer will skip to line 50 and print the statement "A EQUALS 15." If A does not equal B, the computer will go to line 30 and test to see if A is greater than B. If A is greater than B, the computer will skip to line 60 and print the statement "A IS GREATER THAN 15." If A is not greater than B or 15, the computer will fall through to the next line, which is line 35. Upon reaching line 35, the computer will print the statement "A IS LESS THAN 15."

The following table shows sample program executions for several input values for A:

Input	Output
A = 5	A IS LESS THAN 15
A = 10	A IS LESS THAN 15
A = 15	A EQUALS 15
A = 20	A IS GREATER THAN 15
A = 25	A IS GREATER THAN 15

The PRINT Statement

The PRINT statement is used for several different purposes: (1) to command the computer to "call up" values that are in storage; (2) to command the computer to print titles, headings, and/or messages; and (3) to command the computer to print the result of a calculation.

The following example of a partial program illustrates how the PRINT statement can be used to "call up" values from storage and have them printed:

```
40  PRINT A,B,C
50  PRINT X,Y,Z
60  PRINT D1, C3, B4
```

When executing the program on page 40, the computer would cause the printer to print the various values called for in each line of the program. The printer would automatically separate the values into predetermined printing zones. Output paper on a printer is divided into five zones as shown in Figure 2-22.

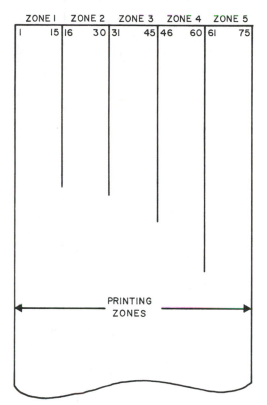

FIGURE 2-22   Printing zones for output.

If, for example, the computer had stored 5, 10, and 15, respectively, as the values for A, B, and C, the output for line 40 would be 5, 10, and 15 (Figure 2-23). The zone lines and column numbers are shown for illustration purposes in Figure 2-23, but would not appear on the actual output paper.

The following example of a partial program illustrates how the PRINT statement can be used to print titles, headings, and/or messages. These things are referred to as *literals* and must be enclosed in quotation marks.

```
30 PRINT "BILL OF MATERIAL"
40 PRINT "14-INCH DOUBLE-TEE ROOF MEMBERS"
50 PRINT "PAGE ONE OF ONE"
```

When the computer actually prints each line, only the words, without the quotation marks, will be printed. The example shown above is part of a program for listing the bill of material for a project in structural drafting. The bill of material will be of all 14-inch double-tee roof members used on a particular job. The output generated by executing lines 30, 40, and 50 is shown in Figure 2-24.

1
15 16
30 31
45 46
60 61
75
5
10
15

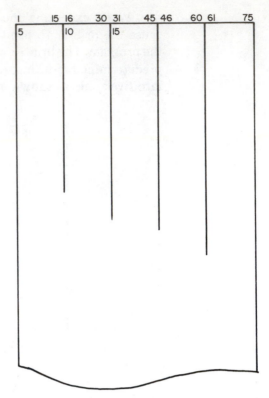

FIGURE 2-23 Sample zoned output.

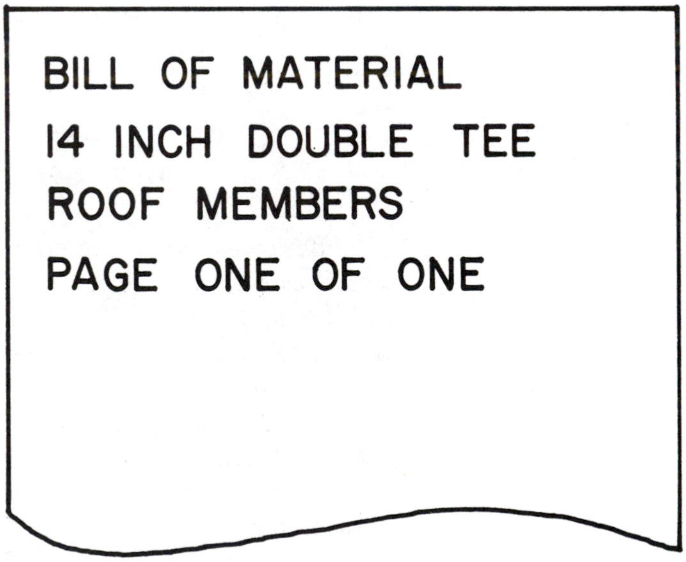

BILL OF MATERIAL
14 INCH DOUBLE TEE
ROOF MEMBERS
PAGE ONE OF ONE

FIGURE 2-24 Sample printout.

The final use for the PRINT statement is to print the result of a mathematical computation that the computer has performed. The following example of a program illustrates how the PRINT statement can be used for this purpose:

```
10 LET A = 10
20 LET B = 15
30 LET C = A + B
40 PRINT C
```

In the example on page 42, the computer would store the value 10 for A. Upon reaching line 20, it would store the value 15 for B. In line 30, the computer would call up the values for A and B, add them together, and store the results in a location named "C." When it reached line 40, the computer would then print the value stored for C, which in this case would be 25.

The GOTO Statement

In writing BASIC programs, the programmer uses IF statements to allow for decisions. IF statements are known as *conditional* statements because if one condition exists, the computer takes a certain type of action, and if another condition exists, it takes another action. Often, the action taken by the computer after an IF statement is to skip to another line in the program and execute that line. The following partial program illustrates that situation:

```
200  IF A > B THEN 100
300  PRINT A
```

An unconditional statement is also available in BASIC language programming. The GOTO statement in BASIC programming is an unconditional statement. This means that it commands the computer to go to another line in the program and sets no conditions. Upon reaching a GOTO statement in a program, the computer goes immediately to the designated line and continues to do so until instructed to stop. The computer may be stopped by an END statement, discussed in the next section.

The following example of a partial program contains a GOTO statement. It shows what would happen if the program were executed without an END statement.

```
PROGRAM

10  PRINT "SAMPLE PROGRAM WITH GOTO STATEMENT"
20  PRINT
30  GOTO 10


PROGRAM EXECUTION

SAMPLE PROGRAM WITH GOTO STATEMENT
SAMPLE PROGRAM WITH GOTO STATEMENT
SAMPLE PROGRAM WITH GOTO STATEMENT
SAMPLE PROGRAM WITH GOTO STATEMENT
SAMPLE PROGRAM WITH GOTO STATEMENT
. . . . . . . . . . . . . . . . . . . . . . . . . . . . . . . . . . . .
```

Because no END statement has been written into the program, the computer will simply continue printing line 10 forever or until the computer is turned off. The following program shows how the GOTO statement might actually be used. It was designed to print a list of the whole numbers from 1 through 50.

```
10  PRINT "WHOLE NUMBERS FROM 1 THROUGH 50"
20  PRINT
30  LET A = 1
40  PRINT A
50  LET A = A + 1
60  PRINT A
70  IF A > 49 THEN 90
80  GOTO 50
90  END
```

An examination of the program line by line will help you begin to understand how BASIC programs work. In line 10, the computer will print the literal title as follows:

WHOLE NUMBERS FROM 1 THROUGH 50

In line 20, the computer will print nothing. This will cause a space between the title and body on the printout. In line 30, the computer will set aside a storage location, name it "A," and place the value "1" in it. In line 40, the computer will print the most current value stored for A, in this case 1. In line 50, the computer will increment the value stored for A by 1. This will make the current value of A equal 2. In line 60, the computer will again print the current value of A, which is now 2. In line 70, the computer will test the current value of A. If it is less than 50, it will proceed to line 80. If it is 50, which is the first value greater than 49, it will proceed to line 90. In line 80, the computer confronts a GOTO statement. This statement will cause the computer to continue returning to line 50, incrementing the value of A by 1, and printing that value until all whole numbers from 1 through 50 have been printed. At this point, the computer will proceed to line 90, where it is stopped by an END statement.

The END Statement

The END statement does exactly what it says — it ends a program. There can be only one END statement in a BASIC program and it must be the last line in the program. In some BASIC programs, the END statement is redundant and can be eliminated. The following short program is an example of this:

```
10  LET A = 5
20  LET B = 10
30  LET C = 20
40  LET D = A + B + C
50  PRINT D
```

In the program above, the computer would perform the computation, print the result, and that would be that. An END statement would not be necessary. However, as was illustrated in the preceding section, programs involving GOTO statements will run on forever unless an END statement is written in.

The READ and DATA Statements

The READ and DATA statements in BASIC language programming must be examined together because that is how they are used in programs. DATA statements are used to list a group of data that will be acted on during program execution. READ statements are used to bring each individual item of data from the DATA statement into position to be acted on.

For example, if a long list of material quantities used in a manufacturing job were to be used in computing the quantities for a new job that is similar to the old one, but four times larger, a simple BASIC program could be written to compute the new quantities. This program would make use of the READ and DATA statements. This program could be written as follows:

```
10  PRINT "QUANTITIES REQUIRED FOR NEW JOB"
20  DATA 25, 62, 6, 47, 12, 19, 22
30  READ A
40  PRINT 4 * A
50  GOTO 30
60  END
```

In line 20 of the program above, the DATA statement, the quantities of various materials used in the first job, are listed. In line 30, the READ statement, the computer is commanded to read them one at a time. Consequently, the computer will read 25, execute line 40 for that value, proceed to line 50, and repeat the process in a continuous loop until all values listed in the DATA statement have been acted on. The completed program execution would provide a printout of materials required for the new job which would appear as follows:

```
QUANTITIES REQUIRED FOR NEW JOB
100
248
24
188
48
76
88
```

The REM Statement

The REM or remark statement is a special BASIC statement that allows comments, reminders, or notations to be written into a program without affecting the output. REM statements appear in a listing of a program, but not in the output that results from executing the program. The following program and its corresponding output illustrate the REM statement principle:

```
 10  REM THIS PROGRAM ILLUSTRATES THE REM STATEMENT
 20  PRINT "ODD WHOLE NUMBERS FROM 1 THROUGH 20"
 30  PRINT
 40  LET A = 1
 50  PRINT A
 60  LET A = A + 2
 70  PRINT A
 80  IF A > 17 THEN 100
 90  GOTO 60
100  END
```

Line 10 has been written into the program to tell program users that the program was written to illustrate how REM statements can be used. Line 10 will have no bearing on program execution or output. It is simply a reminder. The printout that would result from executing this program would appear as follows:

```
ODD WHOLE NUMBERS FROM 1 THROUGH 20
1
3
5
7
9
11
13
15
17
19
```

Special BASIC Characters

The BASIC symbols used for such mathematical comparisons as "less than," "greater than," "equal to," and so on, were presented earlier. In addition to these, there are a number of other special symbols used in BASIC language programming. These special symbols and their respective uses are:

Character		Use
+	(plus symbol)	Addition
–	(minus symbol)	Subtraction
/	(slash symbol)	Division
*	(asterisk symbol)	Multiplication
( )	(parentheses symbols)	Mathematical grouping
" "	(quotation symbols)	Printing literals

SUMMARY AND REVIEW

- Computers represent a very significant technological break-through. However, like all machines, they can only do what human beings make them do.

- Computers are given instructions through a program which is a step-by-step set of commands which tell it what to do.

- Computer programmers are people especially trained to write programs in languages that computers can understand.

- The key to the versatility of a computer system is the software.

- The three most common problem-solving computer languages are FORTRAN, COBOL, and BASIC.

- Before writing a program, a computer programmer must do three things: (1) develop a thorough understanding of the task to determine if it can be feasibly performed by a computer; (2) determine the capabilities of the computer which will be used to perform the task; and (3) determine exactly what the end product or output is to be.

- The steps used by a programmer in actually writing a computer program are problem analysis, determination of the method of solution, flowcharting, coding, translation, debugging, and documentation.

- There are two types of flowcharts: systems flowcharts and program flowcharts.

- Systems flowcharts are prepared in such a way that processing steps are read from top to bottom and left to right.

- A program flowchart is a pictorial representation of the steps necessary to solve a problem or perform a task.

- A program flowchart has several uses: as the starting point in writing a program, as a reference in debugging a program, and as documentation of a program.

- Mathematical comparisons may be made in a program flowchart by using the appropriate symbol: equal to ($=$), greater than ($>$), less than ($<$), greater than or equal to ($>=$ or $\geqslant$), and less than or equal to ($<=$ or $\leqslant$).

- In order to be used as a problem-solving tool, the computer must be given a program for instructions and a set of data to operate on.

- The acronym BASIC stands for Beginners All-Purpose Symbolic Instruction Code.

- The most frequently used statements in BASIC language programming are LET, IF, PRINT, GOTO, READ, DATA, REM, and END.

- Several special symbols are used in writing BASIC programs: addition ($+$), subtraction ($-$), division ($/$), multiplication ($*$), mathematical grouping $[\,(\,)\,]$, and printing literals (" ").

SELF-TEST   Directions

Respond to all questions without referring to the chapter. Once all questions have been completed, check each question by referring to the appropriate section of the chapter. Reread those portions of the chapter covering any questions that you answered incorrectly before proceeding to the next chapter.

1. Indicate whether each of the following statements is true or false.
   a. Computers have become so technologically advanced that they will soon be able to operate without any human help.
   b. The key to the versatility of a computer system is the software.
   c. Systems flowcharts are read from bottom to top and left to right.

2. Define the following terms: program; computer programmers.

3. Match the following phrases in the left-hand column with their corresponding symbol in the right-hand column.

   _____ Equal to   a. $\leq$
   _____ Greater than   b. $<$
   _____ Less than   c. $=$
   _____ Greater than or equal to   d. $\geq$
   _____ Less than or equal to   e. $>$

4. The computer requires two things before it can be used as a problem-solving tool. Name these two things.

5. There are eight frequently used statements in BASIC language programming. What are they?

6. What are the three most common problem-solving computer programming languages?

7. There are two types of flowcharts in computer programming. What are they?

8. Name three ways in which a program flowchart might be used.

9. The acronym BASIC stands for what?

10. There are seven different steps used in actually writing a computer program. What are they?

11. Before writing a computer program, a programmer must first do three things. What are they?

12. Sketch the following systems flowcharting symbols: card file; punched card; manual operation; display; document; sort.

13. Sketch the following program flowcharting symbols: process; preparation; annotation; decision.

14. Write a short BASIC program that illustrates the use of the LET, IF, PRINT, GOTO, and END statements.

15. Write a short BASIC program that illustrates the use of the READ, DATA, and REM statements.

3

COMPUTER-RELATED MATH

OBJECTIVES   Upon completion of this chapter, you will be able to:

1. Explain the binary numbering system.
2. Convert binary numbers to decimal form.
3. Convert decimal numbers to binary form.
4. Add and subtract binary numbers.
5. Perform the basic operations of Boolean algebra.

Drafters are accustomed to performing mathematical calculations using decimal or base 10 numbers. Base 10 numbers are those of the form constructed of digits from 0 through 9. For example, using base 10 numbers an architectural drafter might compute the square footage of a building. Civil drafters compute closure, distances, curve data, and traverse data using base 10 numbers. All drafting fields have some type of math inherent in them and all have traditionally used base 10 numbers.

In addition to having the math skills required in their specific drafting fields, computer drafting technicians should also be familiar with computer-related math. Computer-related math includes the binary numbering system and Boolean algebra. The purpose of this chapter is to help drafters become proficient in the fundamentals of computer-related math.

**DECIMAL AND
BINARY NUMBERS**
The base or "radix" of the decimal numbering system is 10. The radix of the binary numbering system is 2. All decimal numbers are represented by one or a combination of 10 numbers, 0 through 9. All binary numbers are represented by one or a combination of two numbers, 0 and 1. The chart in Figure 3-1 shows the binary equivalents for decimal numbers 1 through 20.

Decimal	Binary	Decimal	Binary
1	1	11	1011
2	10	12	1100
3	11	13	1101
4	100	14	1110
5	101	15	1111
6	110	16	10000
7	111	17	10001
8	1000	18	10010
9	1001	19	10011
10	1010	20	10100

FIGURE 3-1   Binary equivalent chart.

In the decimal numbering system, each digit carries a certain "weight" depending on its position (Figure 3-2). For example, in Figure 3-2, the 3 in the "tens" position is actually equal to 3 $\times$ 10 or 30. The 3 in the "hundreds" position is actually equal to 3 $\times$ 100 or 300. Therefore, in the decimal numbering system, the value of a particular digit is found by multiplying that digit times the weight of its position.

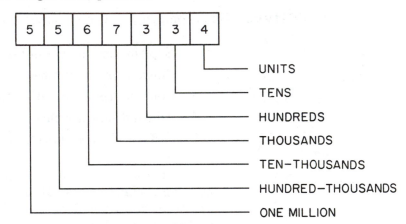

FIGURE 3-2   Decimal weight chart.

Digit positions carry weight in any numbering system. Regardless of the system, the weight of a digit position can be found by multiplying the weight of the digit position immediately to the right by the radix of the numbering system (10 for the decimal numbering system and 2 for the binary numbering system). Figure 3-2 contains a weight chart for the decimal numbering system. Figure 3-3 contains a similar chart for the binary numbering system. Notice from the charts that whereas the positions increase in multiples of 10 in the decimal system, they increase in multiples of 2 in the binary system.

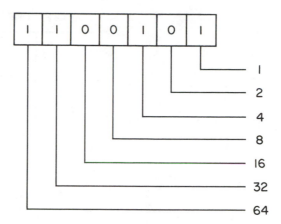

FIGURE 3-3 Binary weight chart.

THE BINARY NUMBERING SYSTEM

To avoid confusion, when working with binary and decimal numbers simultaneously, the radix is placed after the number. For example, the binary number 1011 can be written $(1011)_2$ to avoid confusing it with the decimal number one thousand and eleven. On the other hand, the decimal number 1011 can be written $(1011)_{10}$ to avoid mistaking it as a binary number.

Drafters should be able to convert back and forth between binary and decimal numbers. In either case, it is a matter of several simple steps.

Converting Decimal Numbers to Binary Numbers

Step 1

Begin by drawing two lines at right angles to form a large "T." This T will serve as the format for the table which will be created in the conversion process (Figure 3-4).

Step 2

Enter the decimal number that is to be converted to binary on the left-hand side of the table as shown in Figure 3-4.

Step 3

Divide the decimal number by 2. Place the answer on the left side of the table immediately under the original number and the remainder on the right side of the table as shown in Figure 3-4. If the division works out evenly and there is no remainder, a zero is placed in the right-hand column.

Step 4

Step 3 is repeated until the last number in the left-hand column is zero as shown in Figure 3-4.

Step 5

The binary number is read from the right side of the table starting at the bottom of the column of numbers and working up to the top as shown in Figure 3-4.

```
      STEP ONE              STEP TWO
  _____      _____
          |                    151 |
          |                        |
          |                        |
          |                        |
          |                        |
          |                        |
          |                        |


     STEP THREE             STEP FOUR
  _____      _____
    151 |  1             151 |  1
     75 |                 75 |  1
        |                 37 |  1
        |                 18 |  0
        |                  9 |  1
        |                  4 |  0
        |                  2 |  0
        |                  1 |  1
        |                  0 |


            STEP FIVE
       _____

        SOLUTION = 10010111
```

FIGURE 3-4 Converting decimal numbers to binary.

Converting Binary Numbers to Decimal Numbers

Step 1

Invert the binary number and write it in column form as shown in Figure 3-5.

Step 2

Beginning at the top of the column, place a multiplication to the right of each digit as shown in Figure 3-5.

Step 3

Beginning again at the top of the column, place the appropriate weight value to the right of each digit as shown in Figure 3-5.

Step 4

Multiply each digit times its corresponding weight value and record the answer as shown in Figure 3-5.

Step 5

Add the new column of multiplication products together and read the decimal number as shown in Figure 3-5.

```
Binary number = 10010111

         1 X      1 =     1
         1 X      2 =     2
         1 X      4 =     4
         0 X      8 =     0
         1 X     16 =    16
         0 X     32 =     0
         0 X     64 =     0
         1 X    128 =   128
                        ────
                         151
```

FIGURE 3-5 Converting binary numbers to decimal.

In addition to being able to convert from decimal to binary, and vice versa, the drafter should also be able to add and subtract binary numbers. In both cases there are some elementary rules that must be learned first.

Adding Binary Numbers

The rules for addition of binary numbers are:

1. $0 + 0 = 0$
2. $0 + 1 = 1$
3. $1 + 0 = 1$
4. $1 + 1 = 10$
5. $10 + 1 = 11$

By applying the rules listed above, binary addition problems can be solved. The following sample problems illustrate the applications of the rules for adding binary numbers:

```
   0 1 1 0 1 0 0      Always begin with the right-
  +1 0 0 1 0 1 0      hand column of numbers.
  ─────────────       This sample illustrates the
   0 1 1 1 1 1 0      application of rules 1, 2,
                      and 3.
```

```
 (1)(1)(1)(1)(1)(1)        Notice in this problem that
    1  0  0  1  0  1  1    the 1 is carried to the next
  + 0  1  1  0  1  0  1    column after each addition.
  ──────────────────       This sample illustrates
  1 0  0  0  0  0  0  0    rule 4.
```

```
 (1)(1)(1)
    1  1  1  1      This sample illustrates rule 5.
  + 0  1  1  1
  ───────────
  1 0  1  1  0
```

Subtracting Binary Numbers

The rules for subtraction of binary numbers are:

1. $0 - 0 = 0$
2. $1 - 0 = 1$
3. $1 - 1 = 0$
4. $10 - 1 = 1$

When confronted with the necessity to subtract 1 from 0, a 1 must be borrowed from the column to the immediate left. The following binary numbers subtraction problem has been broken down into a step-by-step solution to illustrate each operation that was performed in solving the problem.

Sample problem with answer

```
  1 1 1 1 0 0
- 0 0 1 1 1 0
  _____
  1 0 1 1 1 0
```

Solution step 1

```
              (0) (10)
    1  1  1  1   0   0
 -  0  0  1  1   1   0
 _____
                 1   0
```

The right-hand column applies rule number 1. The second column from the right requires a borrow from the column to its immediate left.

Solution step 2

```
           (10) (10) (10)
    1  1  1   1    0    0
 -  0  0  1   1    1    0
 _____
           1   1    1    0
```

The third and fourth columns from the right require borrows from the columns to their immediate left.

Solution step 3

```
       (0) (10) (10) (10)
   1  1  1   1    0    0
-  0  0  1   1    1    0
_____
      0   1    1    1    0
```

Because the fourth column from the right borrowed 1, the fifth column became 0 and applied the first rule of subtracting binary numbers.

Solution step 4

$$
\begin{array}{cccccc}
(0) & (10) & (10) & (10) & & \\
1 & 1 & 1 & 1 & 0 & 0 \\
-0 & 0 & 1 & 1 & 1 & 0 \\
\hline
1 & 0 & 1 & 1 & 1 & 0 \\
\end{array}
$$

The final column, which is the farthest from the right, is solved by applying the second rule of subtracting binary numbers.

BASIC OPERATIONS OF BOOLEAN ALGEBRA

In studying Boolean algebra, we are concerned with constants, variables, and operations. The three basic operations of Boolean algebra studied in this chapter are INVERSION, AND, and OR.

A constant is anything with a fixed or unchanging value. For example, the number 7 is a constant because it always represents 7. Other numbers, such as 1, 2, 3, 4, 5, 6, . . . , are also constants in conventional algebraic terms. However, in Boolean algebra there are only two constants: 0 and 1.

A variable is anything with a nonfixed or changeable value. For example, in the conventional algebraic expression $A + B$, there are many values that could be substituted for A and B. However, in Boolean algebra there are only two possible values for variables: 0 and 1.

Operations are the various mathematical ways of acting on constants and variables. Conventional algebraic operations include addition, subtraction, multiplication, and division. There are also a number of different mathematical operations in Boolean algebra. The three most basic operations in Boolean algebra are INVERSION, AND, and OR. When Boolean algebra is applied to logic design, these three operations can be used to describe the action of the three most common logic blocks: the INVERTER block (also referred to as a NEGATOR or NOT block), the AND block, and the OR block. Figure 3-6 presents the symbols recommended by the American National Standards Institute (ANSI) for the INVERTER, AND, and OR blocks.

FIGURE 3-6 Logic symbols.

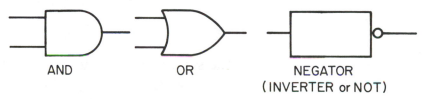

AND   OR   NEGATOR
                          (INVERTER or NOT)

Inversion Operation

The inverse of 1 is written $\bar{1}$. The inverse of 0 is written $\bar{0}$. A value or a variable may be inverted by placing the "bar" sign (–) over it. For example, the symbol for the inverse of A is $\bar{A}$. Variables have two forms, the "true" form and the "inverted" form. The following examples illustrate the principle of INVERSION:

$$\bar{1} = 0$$
$$\bar{0} = 1$$
If A = 1, then $\bar{A}$ = 0   If A = 0, then $\bar{A}$ = 1

The principle of INVERSION can be used in logic design to describe the operation of an INVERTER block. Figure 3–7 demonstrates the principle of INVERSION as it applies in logic design.

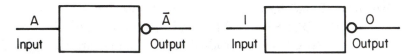

FIGURE 3-7   INVERSION principle.

AND Operation

The symbol for the AND operation is a period or dot raised to the half-height of a line. For example, the operation A AND B is written A ∘ B. There are four basic rules of the AND operation with which the computer drafting technician should be familiar:

$$0 \cdot 0 = 0$$
$$0 \cdot 1 = 0$$
$$1 \cdot 0 = 0$$
$$1 \cdot 1 = 1$$

The first rule actually reads: "Zero ANDed with zero equals zero." Rule two reads: "Zero ANDed with one equals zero." Notice that when ANDing two constants together, both must be 1 in order for the result to be 1. If more than two constants are ANDed together, they all must be 1 for the result to be 1. The following principles illustrate this principle:

$$0 \cdot 0 \cdot 0 \cdot 1 = 0$$
$$1 \cdot 1 \cdot 1 \cdot 1 = 1$$

Figure 3–8 illustrates the AND principles as applied to logic design.

OR Operation

The symbol for the OR operation is a plus sign (+). For example, the operation A OR B is written A + B. There are four basic rules

FIGURE 3-8   AND principle.

of the OR operation with which the computer drafting technician should be familiar:

$$0 + 0 = 0$$
$$0 + 1 = 1$$
$$1 + 0 = 1$$
$$1 + 1 = 1$$

The first rule above reads: "Zero ORed with zero equals zero." The second rule reads: "Zero ORed with one equals one." Notice that when ORing two constants together, if either one of them is 1, the result will be 1. If more than two constants are ORed together, the result will be 1 if any of them is 1. The following examples illustrate this principle:

$$0 + 1 + 0 + 0 = 1$$
$$0 + 0 + 0 + 0 = 0$$

Figure 3-9 illustrates the OR principle as applied to logic design.

FIGURE 3-9   OR principle.

CONSTRUCTING TRUTH TABLES

A truth table is a table that contains a list of the values of a Boolean expression for all possible combinations of values of variables in an expression. Truth tables are used for determining if two expressions are equivalent and in proving simple one-variable theorems.

Constructing a truth table is a simple operation because all variables in a Boolean expression must assume one of two values: 0 or 1. For the purpose of illustration, the truth table for the Boolean expression $A + B + C$ has been constructed below in a step-by-step progression. Notice that the left side of the table is constructed first and then the right side is added.

Step 1

Begin with the variable C. It has two possible values, 1 and 0. Begin the table by placing the two possible values for C under it in column form as shown in Figure 3-10.

FIGURE 3-10

Step 2

Place the next variable, B, to the left of C. Since B must also be either 1 or 0, there are now four possible combinations of A and B. They are:

$$B = 0 \quad \text{and} \quad C = 0$$
$$B = 0 \quad \text{and} \quad C = 1$$
$$B = 1 \quad \text{and} \quad C = 0$$
$$B = 1 \quad \text{and} \quad C = 1$$

Place the possible values for B in column form under B in the table and repeat the values of C (Figure 3-11).

Step 3

Place the next variable, A, to the left of B. Since A must be either 1 or 0, there are now eight possible combinations of A, B, and C. They are:

$$A = 0, \quad B = 0, \quad \text{and} \quad C = 0$$
$$A = 0, \quad B = 0, \quad \text{and} \quad C = 1$$
$$A = 0, \quad B = 1, \quad \text{and} \quad C = 0$$
$$A = 0, \quad B = 1, \quad \text{and} \quad C = 1$$
$$A = 1, \quad B = 0, \quad \text{and} \quad C = 0$$
$$A = 1, \quad B = 0, \quad \text{and} \quad C = 1$$
$$A = 1, \quad B = 1, \quad \text{and} \quad C = 0$$
$$A = 1, \quad B = 1, \quad \text{and} \quad C = 1$$

Place the possible values for A in column form under A and repeat the values for B and C as shown in Figure 3-11.

A	B	C
0	0	0
0	0	1
0	1	0
0	1	1
1	0	0
1	0	1
1	1	0
1	1	1

FIGURE 3-11

Step 4

The left side of the truth table is now completed and the right side may be developed. This is accomplished by applying the appropriate operation to each row one at a time. The truth table in Figure 3-11 was constructed for an ORed expression. This means that the result of the first line would be 0 and all of the remaining lines would be 1, as shown in Figure 3-12.
If the expression had been and ANDed expression, the completed truth table would appear as shown in Figure 3-13.

The truth table in Figure 3-14 shows all of the combinations for Boolean algebra expressions containing up to five variables for both the AND and the OR operations.

A	B	C	D
0	0	0	0
0	0	1	1
0	1	0	1
0	1	1	1
1	0	0	1
1	0	1	1
1	1	0	1
1	1	1	1

FIGURE 3-12

A	B	C	D
0	0	0	0
0	0	1	0
0	1	0	0
0	1	1	0
1	0	0	0
1	0	1	0
1	1	0	0
1	1	1	1

FIGURE 3-13

5 A	4 B	3 C	2 D	E	and	or
0	0	0	0	0	0	0
0	0	0	0	1	0	1
0	0	0	1	0	0	1
0	0	0	1	1	0	1
0	0	1	0	0	0	1
0	0	1	0	1	0	1
0	0	1	1	0	0	1
0	0	1	1	1	0	1
0	1	0	0	0	0	1
0	1	0	0	1	0	1
0	1	0	1	0	0	1
0	1	0	1	1	0	1
0	1	1	0	0	0	1
0	1	1	1	0	0	1
0	1	1	1	1	0	1
1	0	0	0	0	0	1
1	0	0	0	1	0	1
1	0	0	1	0	0	1
1	0	0	1	1	0	1
1	0	1	0	0	0	1
1	0	1	0	1	0	1
1	0	1	1	0	0	1
1	0	1	1	1	0	1
1	1	0	0	0	0	1
1	1	0	0	1	0	1
1	1	0	1	0	0	1
1	1	0	1	1	0	1
1	1	1	0	0	0	1
1	1	1	0	1	0	1
1	1	1	1	0	0	1
1	1	1	1	1	1	1

FIGURE 3-14 Truth table for five variable expression.

SUMMARY AND REVIEW

- Drafters are accustomed to performing mathematical operations using decimal or base 10 numbers. In addition to understanding the decimal numbering system, computer drafting technicians should also be familiar with the binary numbering system.

- The radix of the decimal numbering system is 10, whereas the radix of the binary numbering system is 2.

- All decimal numbers are represented by one or a combination of 10 numbers (0 through 9). For example, 16, 1, 4, 6, 739, and 43678.92 are all decimal numbers.

- All binary numbers are represented by one or a combination of two numbers (0 and 1). For example, 10, 1011, 11101, 0011101, and 1101 are all examples of binary numbers.

- Regardless of the numbering system, all digits in a number carry a certain "weight," depending on their position. For example, the 5 in 351 carries a weight of 10 and its value can be found as follows: 5×10.

- Some binary and decimal numbers look alike. To avoid confusion, the radix can be added to the number. For example, binary 101 can be written $(101)_2$ and decimal 101 can be written $(101)_{10}$.

- To be able to add binary numbers, the drafter must memorize five rules: $0 + 0 = 0$, $0 + 1 = 1$, $1 + 0 = 1$, $1 + 1 = 10$, and $10 + 1 = 11$.

- To be able to subtract binary numbers, the drafter must memorize four rules: $0 - 0 = 0$, $1 - 0 = 1$, $1 - 1 = 0$, and $10 - 1 = 1$.

- In studying Boolean algebra, the student is concerned with three things: constants, variables, and operations.

- A constant is anything with a fixed or unchanging value. For example, the number 5 is a constant because it always represents the same value, five.

- A variable is anything with a nonfixed or changeable value. For example, in the expression $A + B$, there are many values which could be substituted for the variables A and B.

- Operations are the various ways of acting on constants and variables. The three basic operations of Boolean algebra are INVERSION, AND, and OR.

- In Boolean algebra, variables have two forms: the true form and the inverted form. The true form of A is A. The inverted form of A is $\overline{A}$.

- The following examples illustrate the principle of INVERSION: $\overline{1} = 0$; $\overline{0} = 1$; if $A = 1$, then $\overline{A} = 0$; and if $A = 0$, then $\overline{A} = 1$.

- The rules of the AND operation can be summarized as: $0 \cdot 0 = 0$, $0 \cdot 1 = 0$, $1 \cdot 0 = 0$, and $1 \cdot 1 = 1$.

- The rules of the OR operation can be summarized as: $0 + 0 = 0$, $0 + 1 = 1$, $1 + 0 = 1$, and $1 + 1 = 1$.

- A truth table is a table of values of a Boolean expression for all possible combinations of values of variables in an expression.

SELF-TEST   Directions

Respond to all questions without referring to the chapter. Once the self-test has been completed, refer to the appropriate sections of the chapter and check your answers. Reread those portions of the chapter that cover areas in which you missed questions before proceeding to the next chapter.

1. Define the following terms: variable; constant; operation; truth table.

2. Indicate whether each of the following statements is true or false.
   a. $\bar{1} = 0$
   b. $\bar{A} = B$
   c. $\bar{1} = \bar{1}$
   d. $0 + 0 = 0$
   e. $1 + 1 = 1$
   f. $\bar{1} = \bar{1}$
   g. $A = \bar{A}$
   h. $0 \cdot 0 = 1$
   i. $0 \cdot 1 = 1$
   j. $0 + 1 = 0$

3. The traditional numbering system that has always been used by drafters is the:
   a. Binary system
   b. Metric system
   c. Decimal system
   d. Boolean system

4. Computer-related math involves a different numbering system called the:
   a. Algebraic system
   b. Binary system
   c. Euclid system
   d. Ohm's system

5. Indicate the numbers in the following lists of numbers which could be both binary and decimal.

100	12.360
27	10002
10	781
65	100110.5
437	47.0001
10111	10101110

6. What is the radix of the decimal system? What is the radix of the binary system?

7. Label the "weight" of each digit in the following decimal number: 34725.

8. Label the "weight" of each digit in the following binary number: 100101101.

9. Without referring to the table in the chapter, convert the following decimal numbers to binary.

3	13
6	15
9	19

10. Without referring to the table in the chapter, convert the following binary numbers to decimal.

    100   1110
    111   10001
    1010   10100

11. In studying Boolean algebra, the drafter is concerned about what three things?

12. What are the three basic operations of Boolean algebra?

13. Perform the following binary additions:

    $1\;0\;0\;1\;1$ $1\;1\;1\;0\;0\;1\;1$
    $\underline{+1\;1\;1\;0\;0}$ $\underline{+0\;1\;1\;0\;1\;0\;0}$

14. Perform the following binary subtractions:

    $1\;1\;1\;1\;1\;1\;0\;1$ $0\;0\;1\;0\;1\;1\;1$
    $\underline{-1\;1\;0\;1\;1\;0\;0\;1}$ $\underline{-0\;0\;0\;1\;0\;1\;0}$

15. Sketch the ANSI recommended symbols for the following: INVERTER block; AND block; OR block.

4

THE COMPUTER
IN DRAFTING

OBJECTIVES Upon completion of this chapter, you will be able to:

1. Present a comprehensive overview of the computer in drafting.
2. Answer questions frequently asked about computer-aided drafting.
3. Explain some of the common applications of the computer in drafting.

OVERVIEW OF COMPUTER-AIDED DRAFTING Computer-aided drafting, or automated drafting as it is also known, began to interest professionals in the field in the early 1970s. Interest continued to grow throughout the 1970s to the extent that the dawning of the 1980s saw widespread acceptance of the computer in drafting worldwide. By 1990, computer-aided drafting will probably be the norm in drafting, even in the smallest companies.

Computer-aided drafting is the latest and most radical of a long list of innovations which have come about over the years in the name of increased productivity. In spite of the complexities often associated with them, computers are really nothing more than tools. Computer-aided drafting involves using the computer as a tool in the design of a product and the development of drawings for that product. In addition, the computer is used for compiling parts lists, bills of material, schedules, and all of the other tasks which together with making drawings, are collectively known as drafting.

Traditionally, much of what drafters do on the job is tedious, laborious, repetitive, and time consuming. Because of this, drafting has always been in a state of fluctuation as new and better tools and techniques were developed to cut down on the amount of time required to perform drafting tasks, thereby making the drafter more productive.

The term "drafting" can be misleading because there are numerous types of drafting, all of which vary substantially from the others. However, there are certain basic skills that are required in all drafting fields. Some of these are:

1. Neat, legible, but fast lettering
2. Neat, fast linework skills
3. Accurate scale use
4. Dimensioning knowledge and skills
5. An understanding of the principles of orthographic projection
6. An understanding of the principles of axonometric projection
7. An understanding of the principles of sectioning
8. An ability to think in three dimensions
9. An ability to "visualize"

Becoming proficient in the basics listed above requires in-depth, highly specialized technical training. Even with this, such things as speed, accuracy, and neatness are not strong points of human beings. Even the best drafters find freehand lettering, manual linework, and accurate scale use to be slow, arduous tasks which add substantially to the amount of time required to prepare the plans for a job.

The inherent slowness of human beings also impedes progress in performing such other tasks as drawing repetitive details, compiling bills of material or parts lists, redrawing lost or ruined originals, doing corrections, and making revisions. These things, coupled with the ever-increasing demands to produce more drawings of better quality in less time, led to the development of computer-aided drafting.

In order to completely understand computer-aided drafting, one must examine it in light of the overall development of drafting over the years. By comparing manual and computer-aided drafting, you will discover that computer-aided drafting is not another type of drafting, nor is it another drafting field. Rather, it is a new and faster way TO DO drafting that involves all drafting fields.

Manual Drafting versus Computer-Aided Drafting

Drafting is one of the oldest occupations. It has been practiced since humankind first felt the need to design, invent, build, or manufacture to better its lot on earth. In fact, the famous artist and inventor Leonardo daVinci was himself an accomplished drafter. Some of his most famous works are intricately detailed plans for his numerous inventions.

Drafting began to flourish as an occupation when industry adopted mass production techniques. Mass production meant that one person might develop an idea, another might design a product based on the idea, several people might manufacture the various parts of the product, several other people might assemble the parts into the finished product, and yet other people might deliver the finished product to its destination. The primary means of communication which threaded all of these components of the overall process together was, and still is, drawings done by drafters.

Over the years, the need for drawings has not changed. However, the tools and techniques used to produce drawings have. At one time, the T-square and lap board were the drafter's main items of hardware (Figure 4-1). As time went by and the need to produce higher-quality drawings faster continued to increase, drafting hardware improved. Parallel bars strung on drafting tables and highly accurate drawing and inking sets became available (Figures 4-2 through 4-4).

FIGURE 4-1   At one time this represented state-of-the-art technology in drafting.

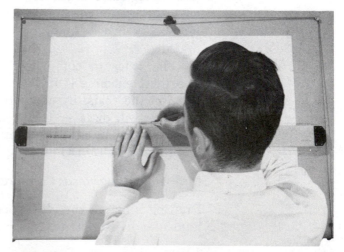

FIGURE 4-2   Parallel bar and drafting table. (Courtesy of Keuffel & Esser Company, Morristown, N.J.)

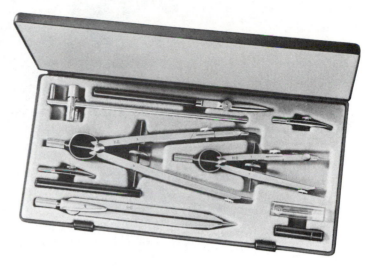

FIGURE 4-3 Mechanical drafting instruments. (Courtesy of Keuffel & Esser Company, Morristown, N.J.)

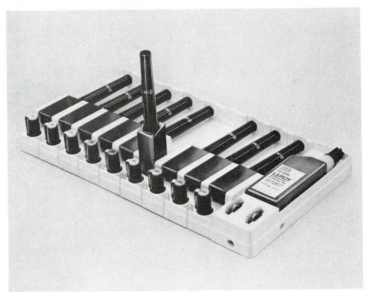

FIGURE 4-4 Inking set. (Courtesy of Keuffel & Esser Company, Morristown, N.J.)

The continued need for ways to increase the drafter's productivity and to improve the quality of drawings led to such innovations as drafting machines and electric erasers (Figures 4-5 and 4-6). Additional timesaving devices such as templates and rub-on transparencies (Figures 4-7 and 4-8) became available. All these things have served to improve the drafter's efficiency and productivity. However, the need for ways to decrease the time requirements of drawings while improving their appearance continues to exist. In fact, it probably always will.

Computer-aided drafting systems are the latest in a long line of technological advances designed to improve on the drafter's capabilities. What makes computer-aided drafting more significant than any of its predecessors is that it represents a conversion from manual to automated drafting.

FIGURE 4-5 Drafting machine and table. (Courtesy of Keuffel & Esser Company, Morristown, N.J.)

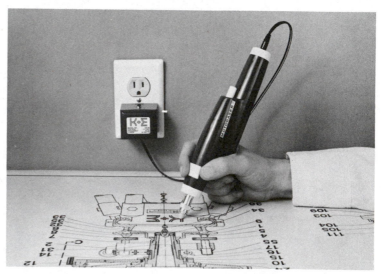

FIGURE 4-6 Electric eraser. (Courtesy of Keuffel & Esser Company, Morristown, N.J.)

FIGURE 4-7 Manual timesaving device still used in architectural drafting.

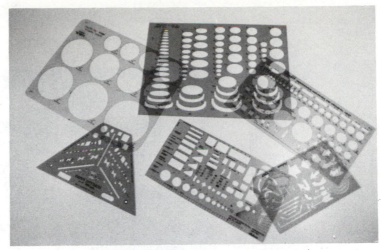

FIGURE 4-8 Templates are used as timesaving devices in every manual drafting application.

Rather than using drafting machines, templates, scales, inking sets, triangles, pencils, and all the other manual drafting tools, computer drafting technicians use such things as digitizing tablets, CRT terminals, plotters, hard-copy units, and printers. These things are some of the pieces of hardware that make up a complete computer drafting system. Figure 4-9 contains a drawing of a typical computer drafting system. Figure 4-10 shows a drafting room that is automated. A close examination of this figure will reveal both the similarities and differences between manual drafting and computer-aided drafting. To appreciate the full impact of computer-aided drafting, one must examine its benefits compared to manual drafting.

FIGURE 4-9 Computer-aided drafting system hardware.

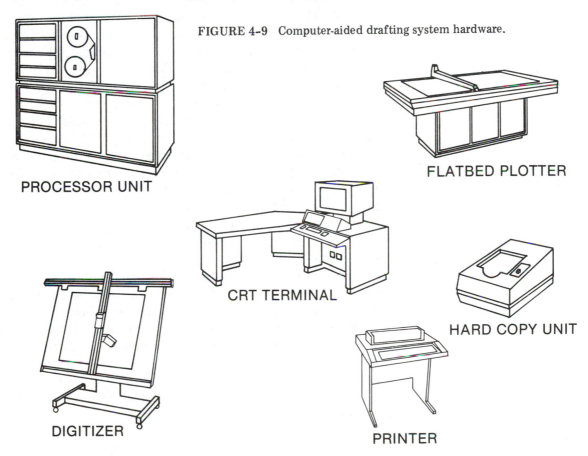

PROCESSOR UNIT

FLATBED PLOTTER

CRT TERMINAL

HARD COPY UNIT

DIGITIZER

PRINTER

FIGURE 4-10 Automated drafting room. (Courtesy of Tektronix Inc.)

Benefits of Computer-Aided Drafting

The single most important benefit of computer-aided drafting is increased productivity. This means that using computer drafting techniques, drafters can do more work in less time. In most drafting applications, the time ratio is 5 : 1 in favor of computer-aided drafting. This means that a drafter, using computer drafting techniques, could do the same amount of work as a manual drafter in one-fifth of the time, or five times as much work in the same amount of time. In some drafting applications, the ratio is as high as 20 : 1. For example, the architectural illustrations in Figures 4-11 and 4-12 were drawn manually. Each drawing took approximately 20 hours to complete. The same drafter, using a computer drafting system, could complete each drawing in approximately 4 hours.

Although increased productivity is the primary benefit of computer-aided drafting, there are several other benefits that are also important. Computer drafting systems can be used for making engineering calculations, cost estimation, material take-offs, project scheduling, and drawings storage. All these tasks represent critical elements in moving a product from the idea stage to the finished-product stage.

The benefits of computer-aided drafting are many. However, there is one distinct disadvantage that must be considered. Many drafters and drafting students feel uneasy about this latest time-saving innovation. There are a number of questions which frequently arise when the topic of discussion is computer-aided drafting. As is the case with any technological change, myths arise and people become concerned. Any study of computer-aided drafting must include an examination of the questions people have about it and factual, realistic answers to these questions.

FIGURE 4-11 Inked drawing done manually is a time-consuming process. (Courtesy of Donald Dishon.)

FIGURE 4-12 Done manually, this drawing took approximately 20 hours to complete. (Courtesy of Donald Dishon.)

Will Computer-Aided Drafting Make Drafters Obsolete?

People tend to fear that automation will eliminate their jobs, and in many cases their fears are justified. However, computer-aided drafting will not eliminate drafting positions. It should be remembered that computers do not make drawings — drafters make drawings using the computer as a tool. The drafter is the critical component of a computer-aided drafting system. The computer will not eliminate the drafter's job. Rather, it will relieve him or her of the more tedious, repetitive aspects of it, thereby allowing more time to be spent on the more important elements of the job.

What Skills Must I Have to Be a Computer Drafting Technician?

The most important skills that a computer drafter needs are the same as those needed by a manual drafter, with the possible exception of such tedious skills as lettering and linework. The computer drafting technician must be knowledgeable in the use of scaling, orthographic projection, axonometric projection, sectioning, dimensioning, visualization, and thinking in three dimensions. In addition to these traditional skills, the computer drafter will need to develop a basic understanding of computers in general, learn to use computer math, become familiar with a computer programming language, learn the various components of a computer drafting system and how they interrelate, and learn how to use such computer drafting system components as digitizing tablets, CRT keyboards, plotters, printers, hard-copy units, cursors, and joysticks.

Do Drafters Write the Programs for Computer Drafting Systems?

Computer programming is a highly specialized field requiring in-depth training. Programmers write the programs used in computer drafting systems. Drafters are usually considered system users. This means that they operate the hardware and supply the computer with the information that it needs to do a job, but they do not develop the actual programs.

What Drafting Fields Are Using Computer-Aided Drafting?

Computer drafting hardware and software has been developed for all the more common drafting applications. Architectural, civil, mechanical, structural, piping, electronics, and pictorial drafting can all be done on computer drafting systems.

How Do Computer Produced Drawings Compare to Manually Produced Drawings?

Computer and manual drawings are very similar. They are laid out in the same format, dimensioned according to the same rules, and arranged in the same order. The primary differences, other than the amount of time required to prepare them, can be found in the quality of linework, lettering, and arrowheads. In these aspects, the computer drawings look far superior to most manually prepared drawings. Figures 4-13 through 4-16 present samples of manually prepared and computer-prepared drawings for comparison.

COMPUTER-AIDED DRAFTING APPLICATIONS

There are a number of different drafting fields that serve as integral components of the building construction industry, manufacturing industry, land development industry, and several other industries. Some of these fields are closely related and even overlap, whereas others are very different from each other. The most common drafting fields are architectural, civil, electronics, mechanical, piping, and pictorial drafting.

All the most common drafting fields and several other less common fields lend themselves to computer-aided drafting. Computer drafting hardware and software is available in the areas of architectural, civil, electronics, mechanical, piping, and pictorial drafting. The following paragraphs will examine computer-aided drafting in each of these application areas on an individual basis and will present samples of drawings done on a computer drafting system.

FIGURE 4-13 Computer-generated drawing of a fireplace detail.

FIGURE 4-14 Manually done drawing of a fireplace detail.

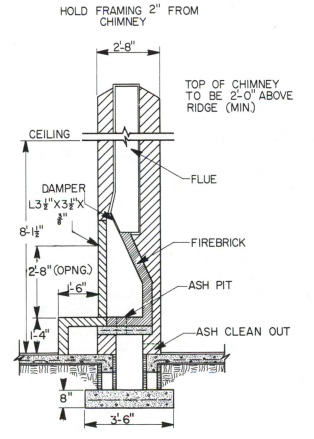

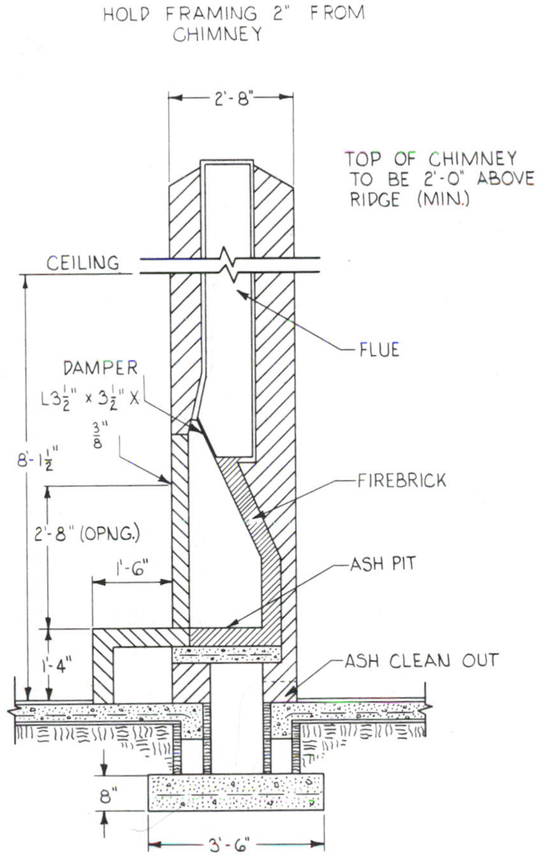

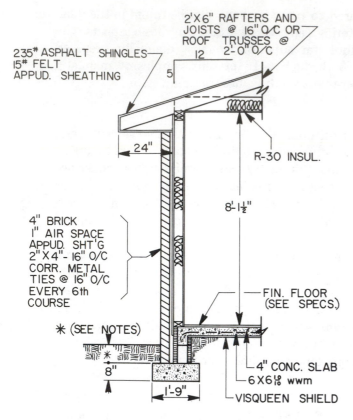

FIGURE 4-15 Computer-generated drawing of a wall section.

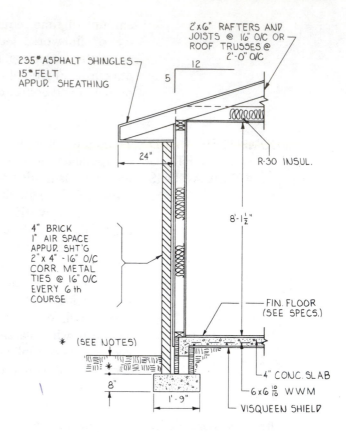

FIGURE 4-16 Manually done drawing of a wall section.

Architectural Drafting

Architectural drafters draw floor plans, foundation plans, construction details, sections, elevations, and plot plans. All of these types of drawings, and other less commonly done drawings, such as furniture plans, can be done on a computer drafting system. Architectural drawings require lettering that is neat and attractive, linework that is clear and consistent, scalework that is accurate, and dimensioning that must be comprehensive and must total out correctly. Architectural drafters must meet all these requirements when preparing drawings and one more: speed.

Computer-aided drafting allows architectural drafters to produce plans that meet all the requirements set forth above. In addition to taking less time to prepare, computer-produced architectural plans are very neat, accurate, and attractive. Figures 4–17 through 4–26 present samples of architectural drawings that were produced on computer-aided drafting systems.

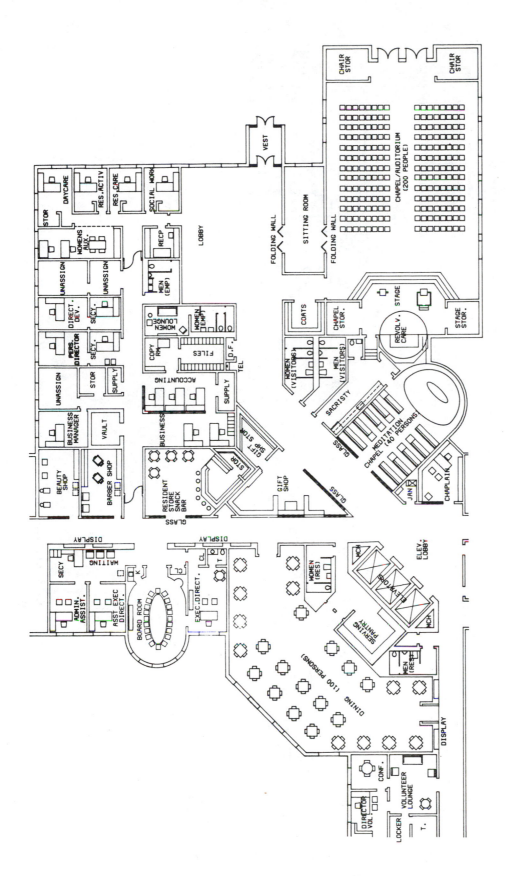

PARTIAL FLOOR PLAN

SCALE 1/8"=1'-0"

FIGURE 4-17 Computer-drawn architectural sample. (Courtesy of Auto-trol Technology Corporation.)

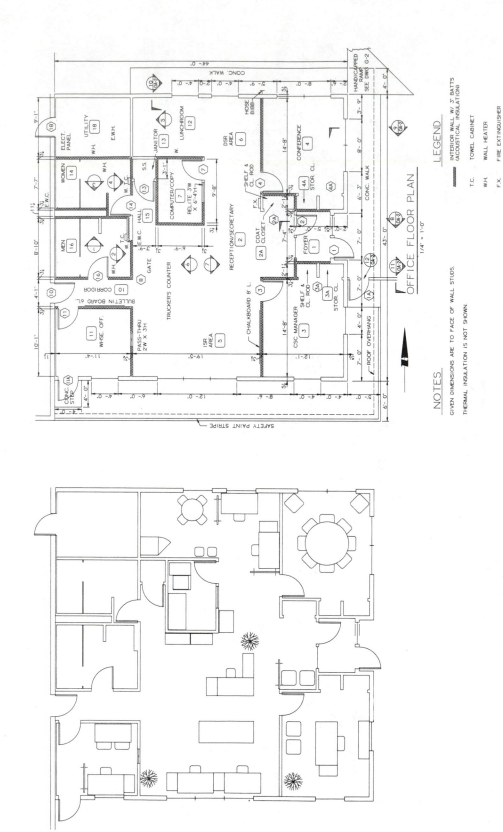

FIGURE 4-18 Computer-drawn architectural sample. (Courtesy of Applicon Incorporated.)

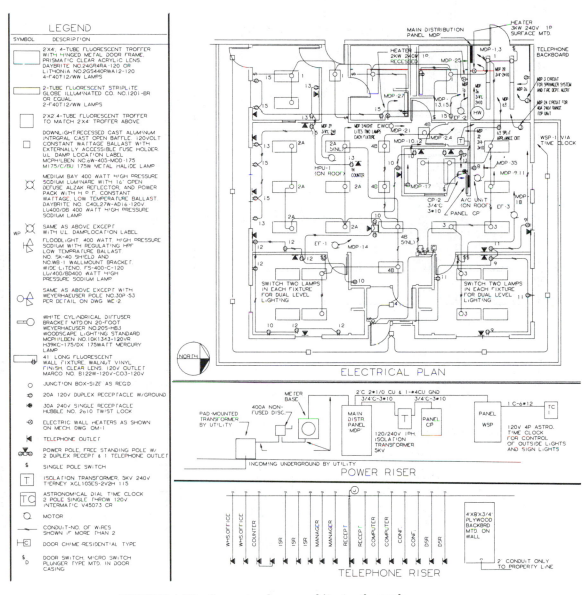

FIGURE 4-19 Computer-drawn architectural sample.
(Courtesy of Applicon Incorporated.)

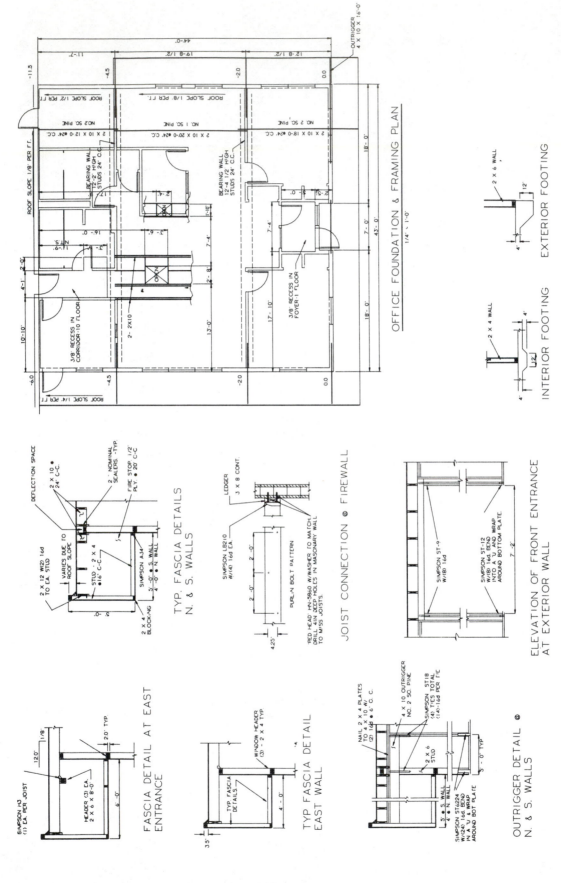

FIGURE 4-20 Computer-drawn architectural sample. (Courtesy of Applicon Incorporated.)

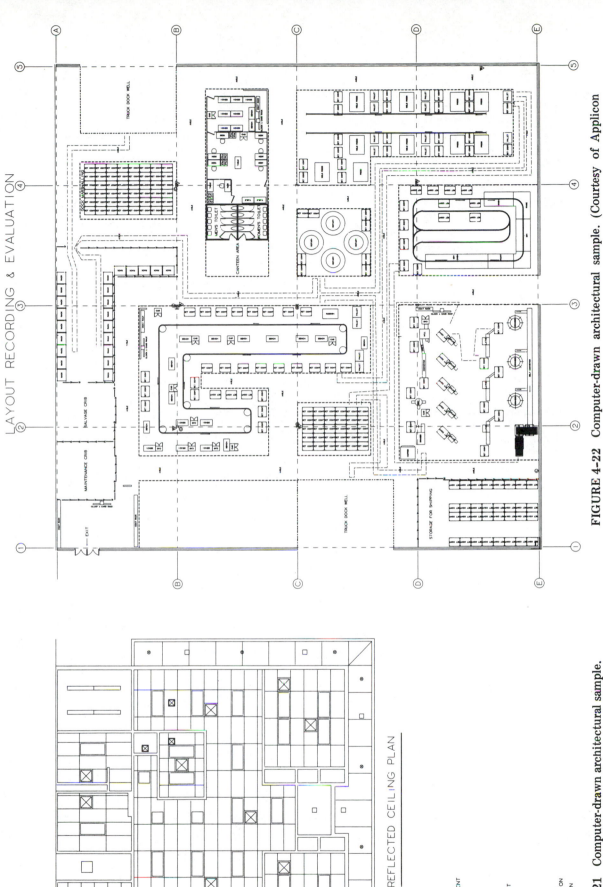

LAYOUT RECORDING & EVALUATION

FIGURE 4-22 Computer-drawn architectural sample. (Courtesy of Applicon Incorporated.)

REFLECTED CEILING PLAN

LEGEND

G.W.B. CEILING

SUSPENDED CEILING

RECESSED FLOURESCENT FIXTURE

SURFACE MOUNTED FIXTURE

RECESSED DOWNLIGHT

AIR DIFFUSER

SOFFIT VENT

FULL-HEIGHT PARTITION

8'-4" HIGH PARTITION

FIGURE 4-21 Computer-drawn architectural sample. (Courtesy of Applicon Incorporated.)

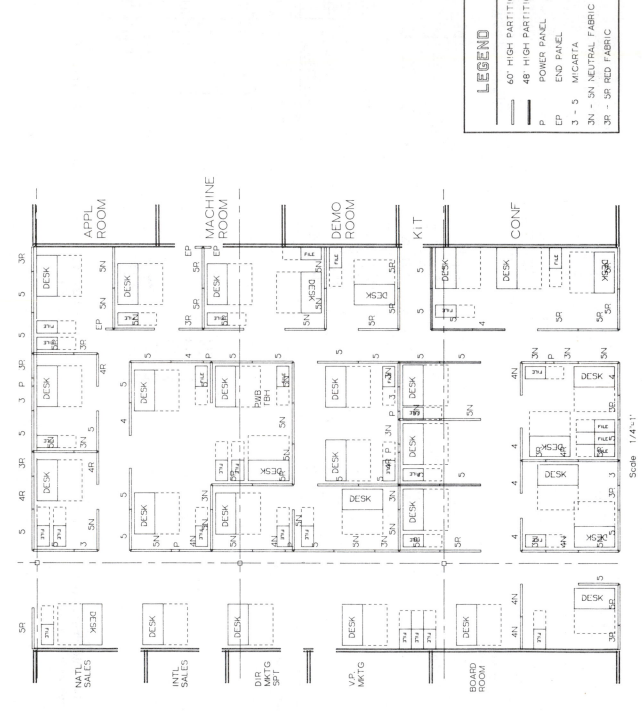

FIGURE 4-23 Computer-drawn architectural sample. (Courtesy of Applicon Incorporated.)

80

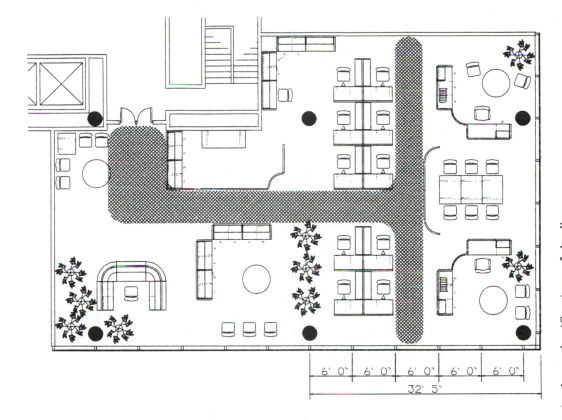

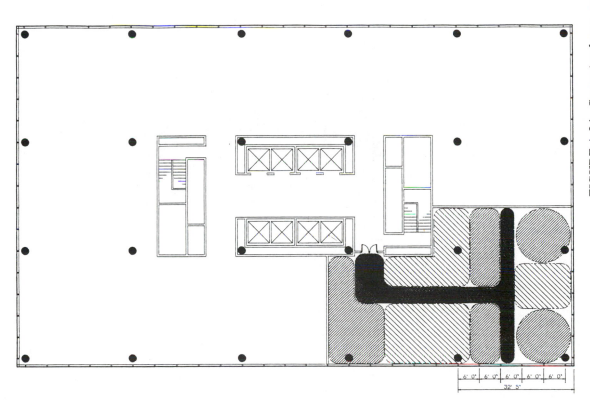

FIGURE 4-24 Computer-drawn architectural sample. (Courtesy of Applicon Incorporated.)

81

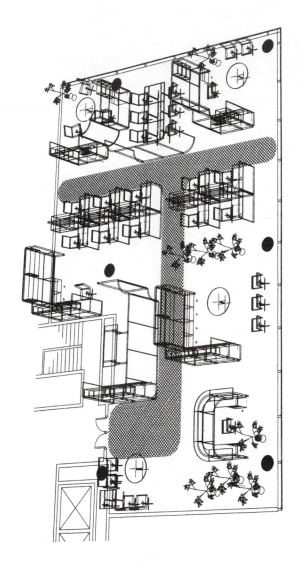

FIGURE 4-25 Computer-drawn architectural sample. (Courtesy of Applicon Incorporated.)

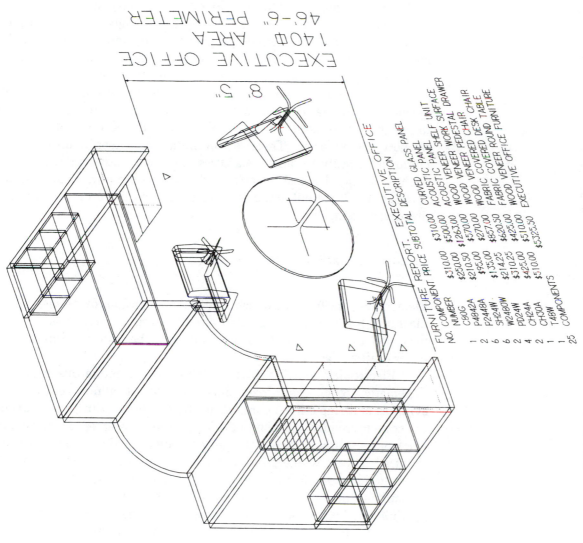

FIGURE 4-26 Computer-drawn architectural sample. (Courtesy of Applicon Incorporated.)

Civil Drafting

Civil drafters may be involved with a wide range of drawing types depending on their employment situation. Civil drafters who work for civil engineering firms or surveyors draw single-lot property plats, subdivision plats, site plans, plot plans, maps, and topographies. Civil drafters working in a county or city engineering department plot easements, road rights-of-way, and water/sewage lines on county or city maps.

Civil drafters are often employed by property appraisal offices, public and private. In these cases, they draw single-lot and multi-lot plats from metes and bounds property descriptions. All these tasks and numerous others normally accomplished manually by civil drafters may be performed on a computer drafting system.

The computer is particularly well suited for use in civil drafting because of the many mathematical computations that must precede drawings and because of the X-Y coordinate methods of plotting property boundaries. Traverse computations, areas computations, curve data, latitudes and departures, and many other mathematical functions may be easily performed on a computer. Figures 4–27 through 4–30 present samples of civil drafting done on a computer drafting system.

Electronics Drafting

Electronics drafters draw schematics, connection diagrams, block diagrams, logic diagrams, printed circuit board layouts, chassis drawings, and pictorials. All these drawings may be produced on a computer drafting system.

Electronics drafting involves the use of numerous symbols. Schematic, block, and logic diagrams consist almost entirely of symbols and single lines connecting the symbols. Prior to the advent of computer-aided drafting, drafters used templates to construct electronics symbols. Templates do cut down on the amount of time required to draw electronics symbols, but even with templates constructing complicated electronics drawings manually is a time-consuming process; whereas with the computer, an electronics symbol may be produced instantly by simply pressing a button.

Computer-aided drafting can reduce the overall time involved in producing a set of drawings by as much as 50%. Time spent in preparing such drawings as schematics or logic diagrams can be cut by as much as 90%. Computer-produced drawings also have the advantage of being more consistent, more accurate, and more attractive. Figures 4–31 through 4–35 present samples of electronics drawings that were done on a computer drafting system.

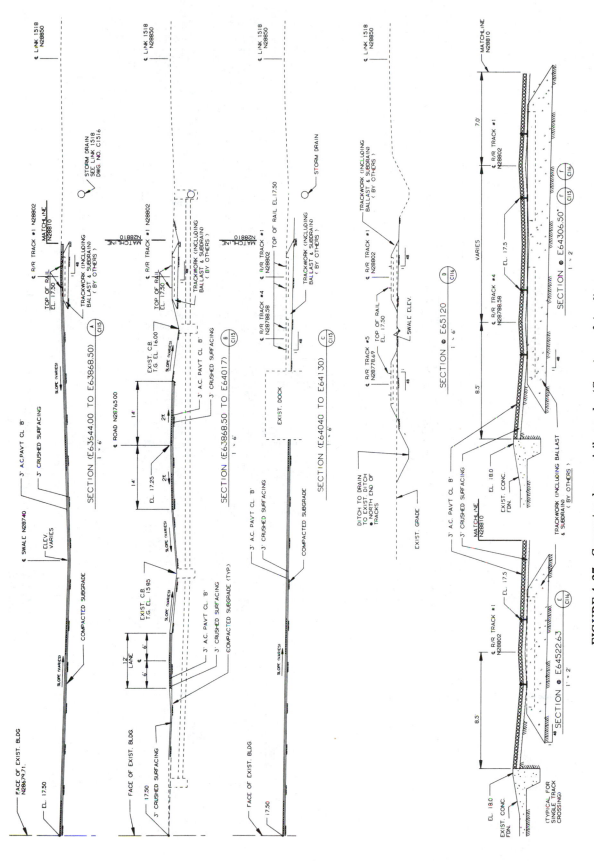

FIGURE 4-27 Computer-drawn civil sample. (Courtesy of Applicon Incorporated.)

85

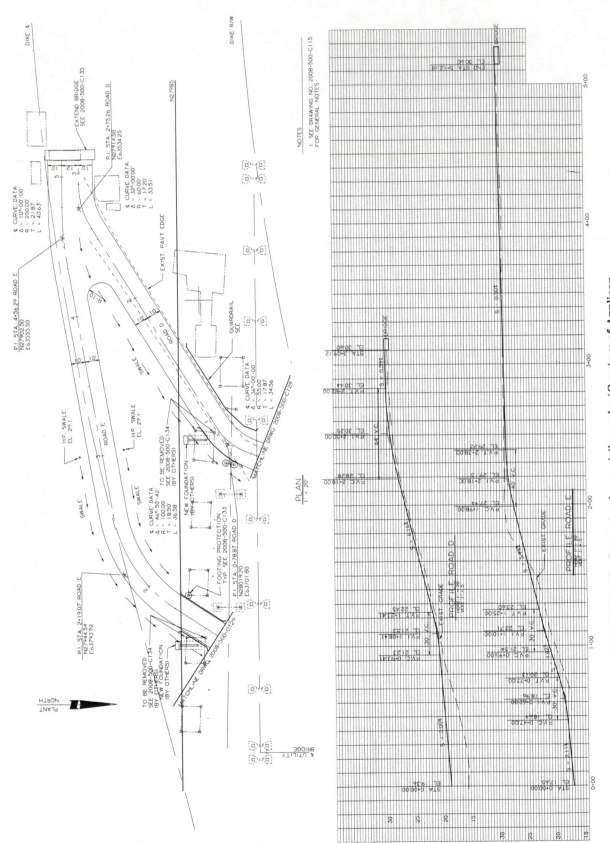

FIGURE 4-28 Computer-drawn civil sample. (Courtesy of Applicon Incorporated.)

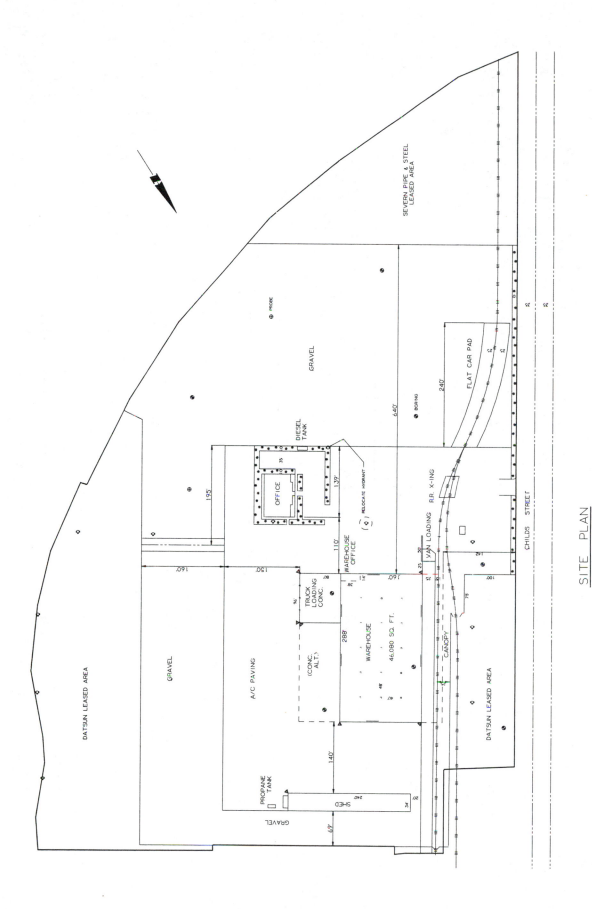

SITE PLAN

1' = 60'

FIGURE 4-29 Computer-drawn civil sample. (Courtesy of Applicon Incorporated.)

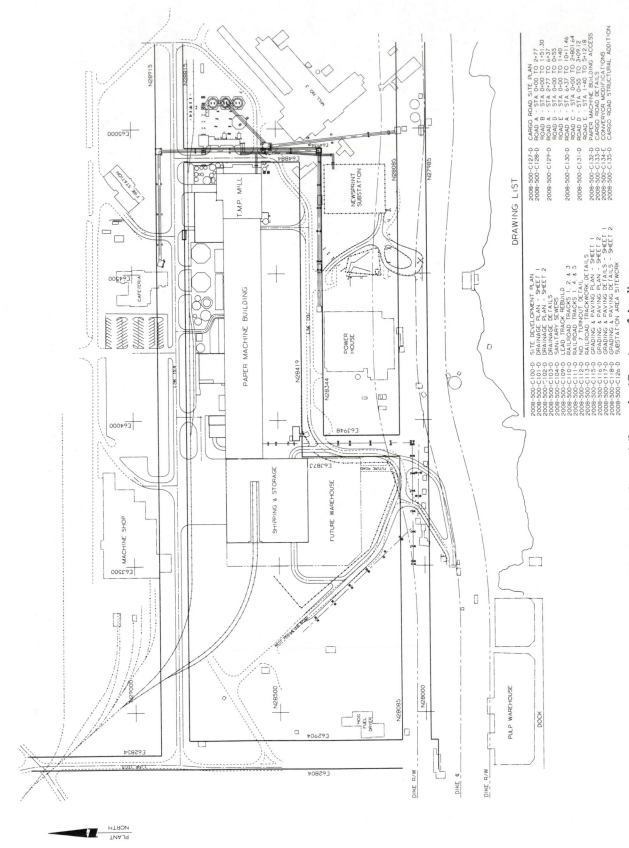

DRAWING LIST

2008-500-C100-D	SITE DEVELOPMENT PLAN
2008-500-C101-D	DRAINAGE PLAN - SHEET 1
2008-500-C102-D	DRAINAGE PLAN - SHEET 2
2008-500-C103-D	DRAINAGE DETAILS
2008-500-C104-D	SANITARY SEWERS
2008-500-C109-D	LEAD TRACK REBUILD
2008-500-C110-D	RAILROAD TRACKS 1, 2, & 3
2008-500-C111-D	RAILROAD TRACKS 1, 4, & 5
2008-500-C112-D	NO. 7 TURNOUT DETAILS
2008-500-C113-D	RAILROAD TRACKWORK DETAILS
2008-500-C115-D	GRADING & PAVING PLAN - SHEET 1
2008-500-C117-D	GRADING & PAVING PLAN - SHEET 2
2008-500-C118-D	GRADING & PAVING DETAILS - SHEET 1
2008-500-C126-D	GRADING & PAVING DETAILS - SHEET 2
	SUBSTATION AREA SITEWORK

2008-500-C127-D	CARGO ROAD SITE PLAN					
2008-500-C128-D	ROAD A	- STA 0-00 TO 2-77				
	ROAD B	- STA 0-00 TO 1-51.30				
2008-500-C129-D	ROAD A	- STA 2-77 TO 6-37				
	ROAD D	- STA 0-00 TO 0-55				
	ROAD E	- STA 0-00 TO 1-40				
2008-500-C130-D	ROAD A	- STA 6-37 TO 10+11.46				
	ROAD C	- STA 0-00 TO 2+801.64				
2008-500-C131-D	ROAD A	- STA 0-55 TO 3+091.2				
	ROAD D	- STA 1-40 TO 5+12.18				
2008-500-C132-D	PAPER MACHINE BUILDING					
2008-500-C133-D	CARGO ROAD DETAILS					
2008-500-C134-E	CONVERYOR MODIFICATIONS					
2008-500-C135-D	CARGO ROAD STRUCTURAL ADDITION					

FIGURE 4-30 Computer-drawn civil sample. (Courtesy of Applicon Incorporated.)

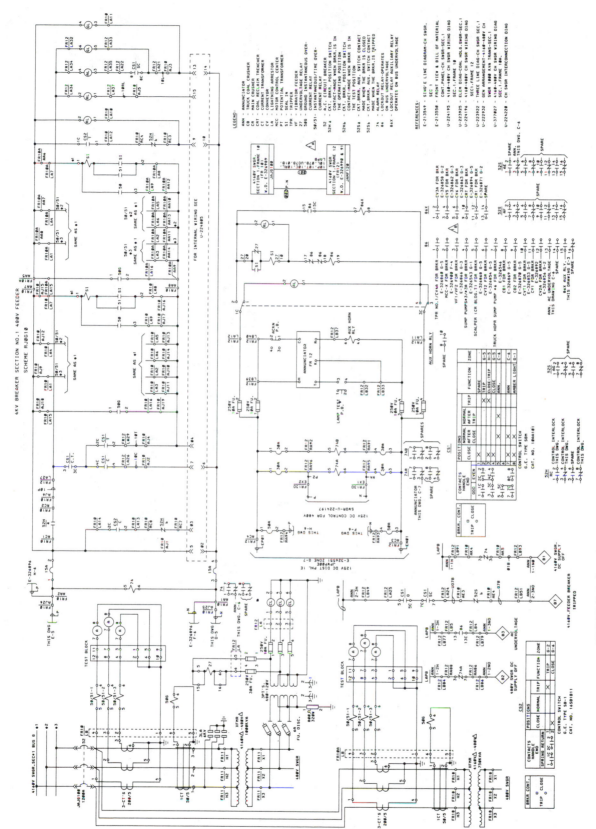

FIGURE 4-31 Computer-drawn electronics sample. (Courtesy of Applicon Incorporated.)

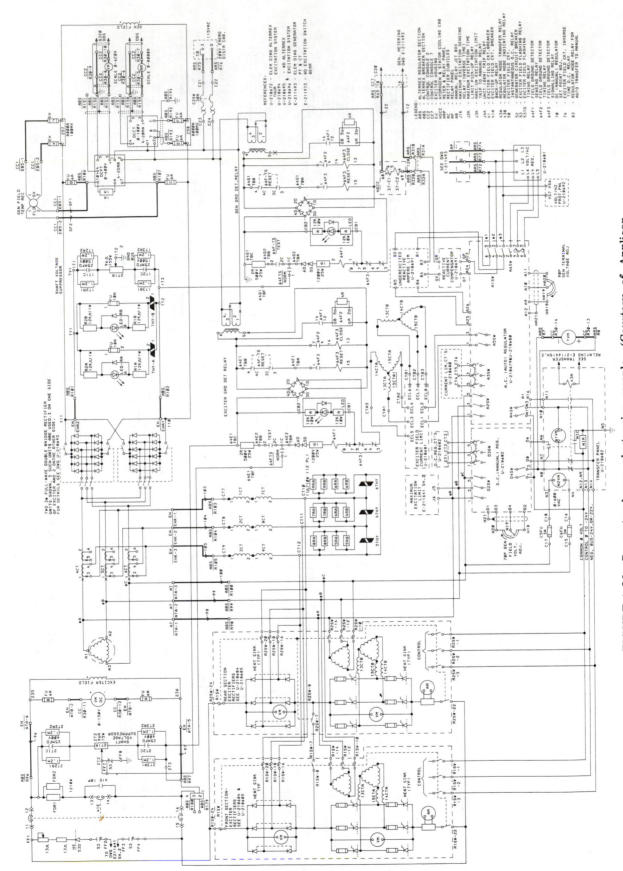

FIGURE 4-32 Computer-drawn electronics sample. (Courtesy of Applicon Incorporated.)

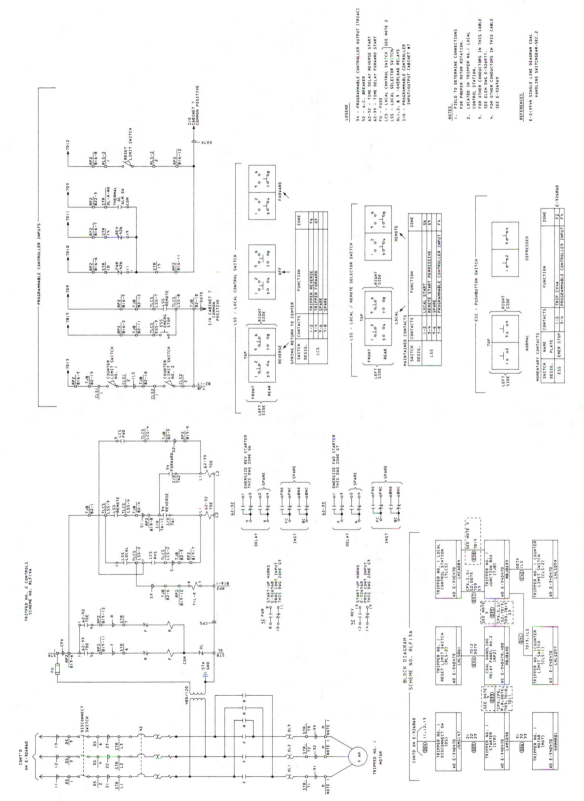

FIGURE 4-33 Computer-drawn electronics sample. (Courtesy of Applicon Incorporated.)

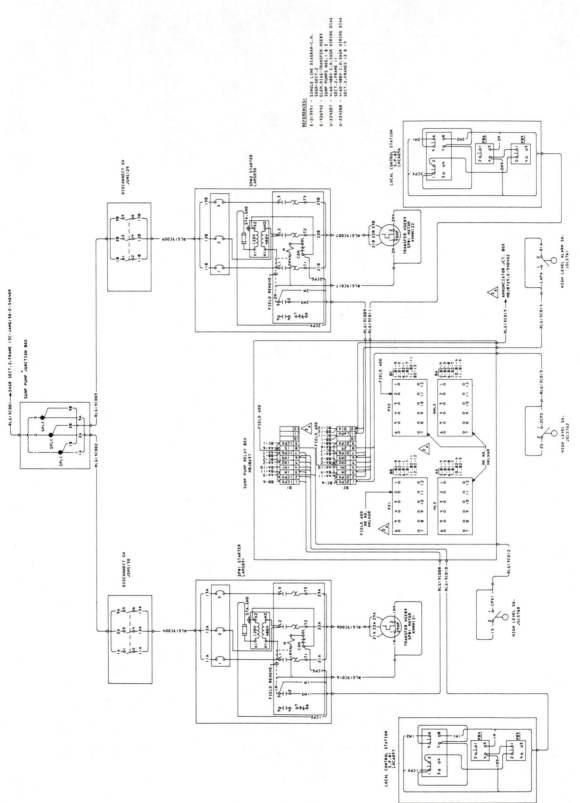

FIGURE 4-34 Computer-drawn electronics sample. (Courtesy of Applicon Incorporated.)

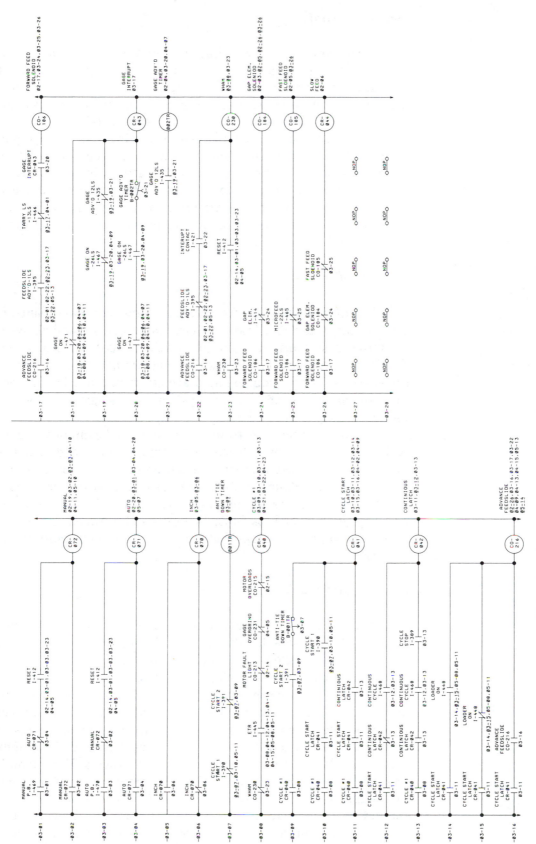

FIGURE 4-35 Computer-drawn electronics sample. (Courtesy of Applicon Incorporated.)

Mechanical Drafting

Mechanical drafters prepare drawings for use in the manufacturing industry. The drawings may be product drawings, jig and fixture drawings, gear drawings, cam drawings, or numerous other types of drawings. In any case, a set of mechanical working drawings contains assemblies, subassemblies, parts lists, and parts details.

Preparing mechanical working drawings involves orthographic or multiview projection, standard dimensioning techniques, lettering, linework, and scalework. A mechanical drafter using computer-aided drafting techniques is able to perform all these tasks faster, neater, and more accurately than a drafter using manual methods. Figures 4–36 through 4–40 present samples of mechanical drawings done on a computer drafting system.

Piping Drafting

Piping drafters draw plans for piping systems, pumping plants, heating systems, water and sewer systems, industrial gas and air systems, oil refinery systems, refrigeration systems, gas lines, and chemical distribution systems. Piping drafting involves constructing single-line schematic drawings, double-line drawings, fitting details, "blowups" of different parts of a piping system, and single- or double-line pictorials.

Piping drafting, due to its frequent use of symbology and pictorials, is particularly well suited to computer-aided drafting techniques. All the tasks listed above can be performed on a computer drafting system. Piping drafters can cut down on the time required to produce single-line schematics by as much as 90% and double-line drawings by as much as 50%. Figures 4–41 through 4–48 present samples of piping drawings that were produced on a computer drafting system.

Pictorial Drafting

Pictorial drafting involves isometric, dimetric, trimetric, oblique, and occasionally orthographic drawings. Although drafters in most fields are occasionally called on to construct pictorials, some specialize in pictorials and become known as illustrators.

Pictorial drafting results in drawings that may be used for sales and marketing purposes, to clarify complicated design situations, or to communicate concepts to people who are unable to read and understand orthographic technical drawings. Creating pictorial drawings manually is a time-consuming, tedious process. For example, if an architect wishes to display three different views of a proposed new building (normal view, bird's-eye view, and worm's-eye view), the drafter would have to construct three complete drawings starting from scratch each time. The same task could be performed on a computer drafting system in less than half of the time.

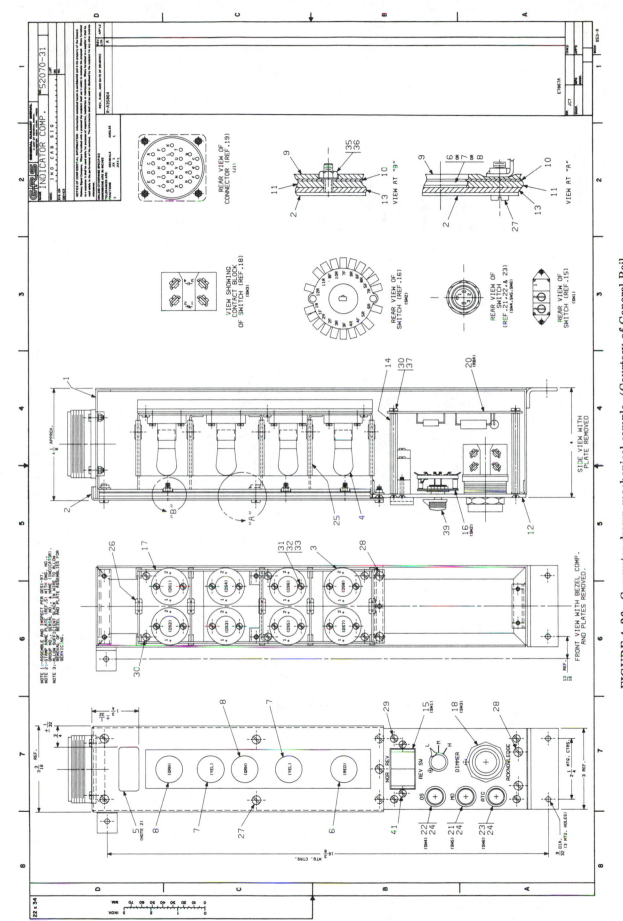

FIGURE 4-36 Computer-drawn mechanical sample. (Courtesy of General Railway Signal Company.)

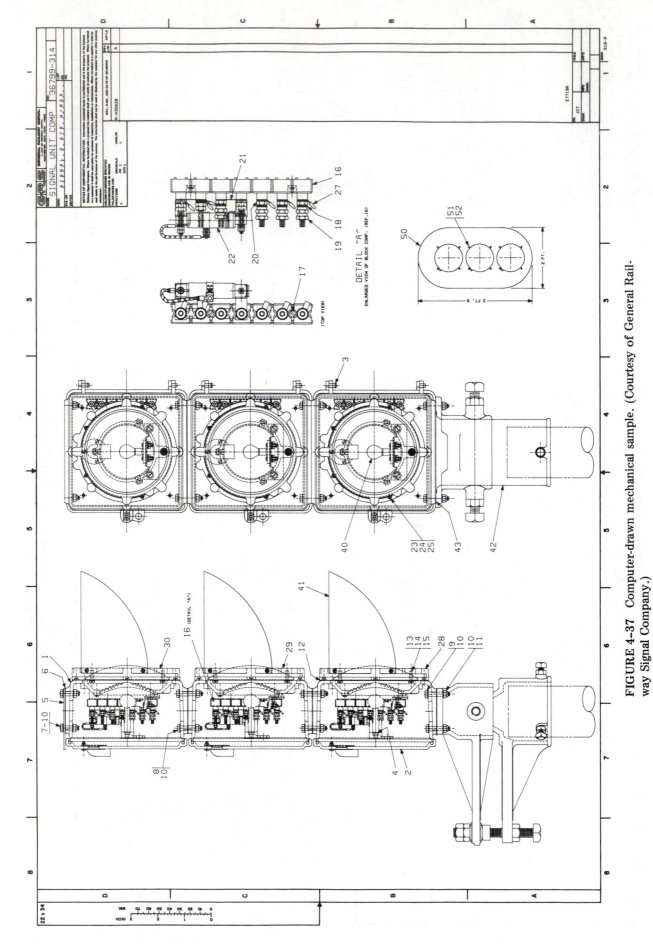

FIGURE 4-37 Computer-drawn mechanical sample. (Courtesy of General Railway Signal Company.)

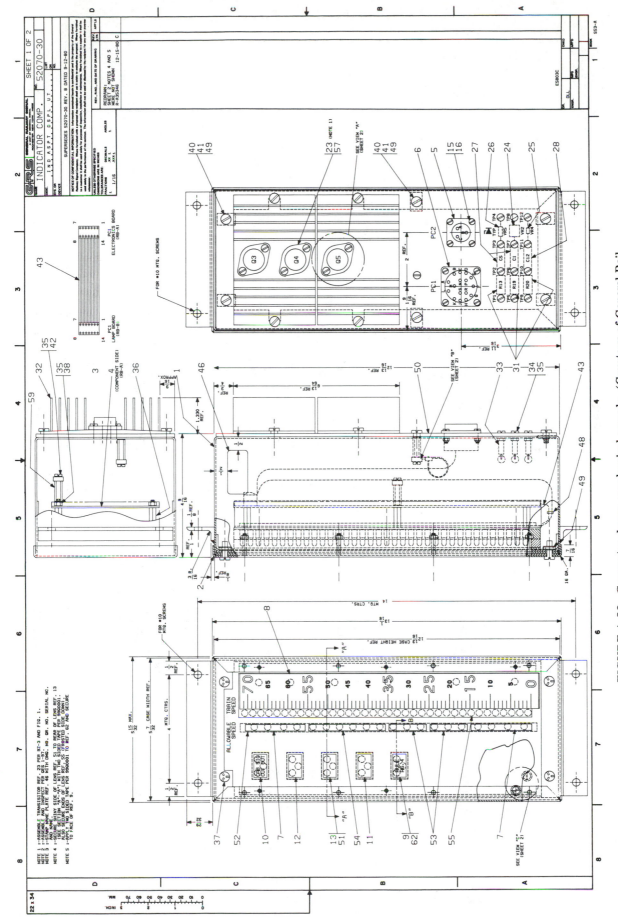

FIGURE 4-38 Computer-drawn mechanical sample. (Courtesy of General Railway Signal Company.)

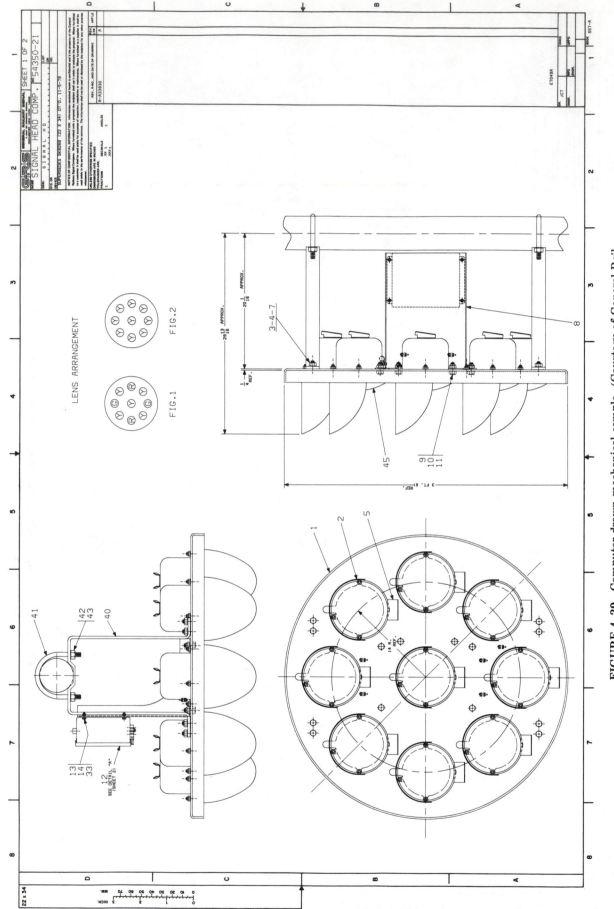

FIGURE 4-39 Computer-drawn mechanical sample. (Courtesy of General Railway Signal Company.)

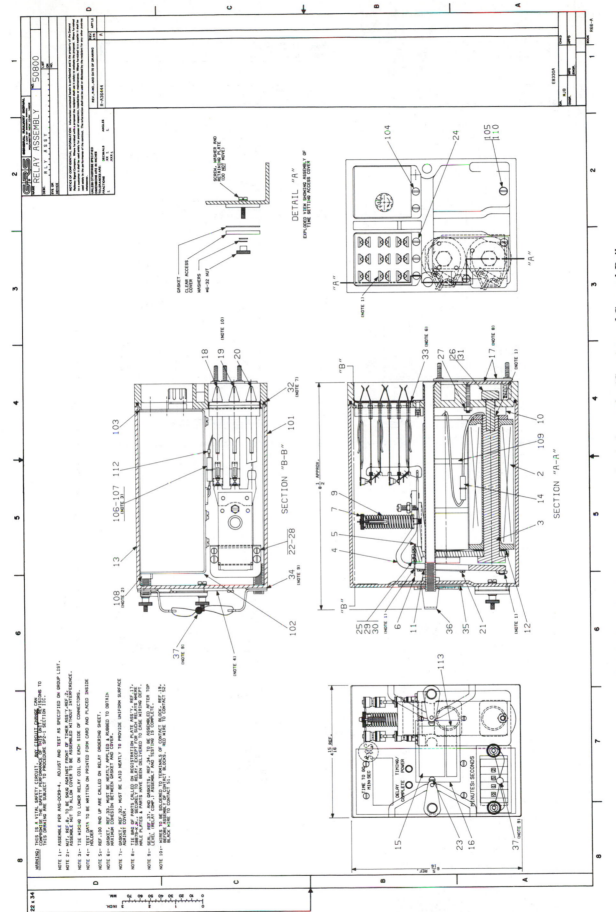

FIGURE 4-40 Computer-drawn mechanical sample. (Courtesy of General Railway Signal Company.)

99

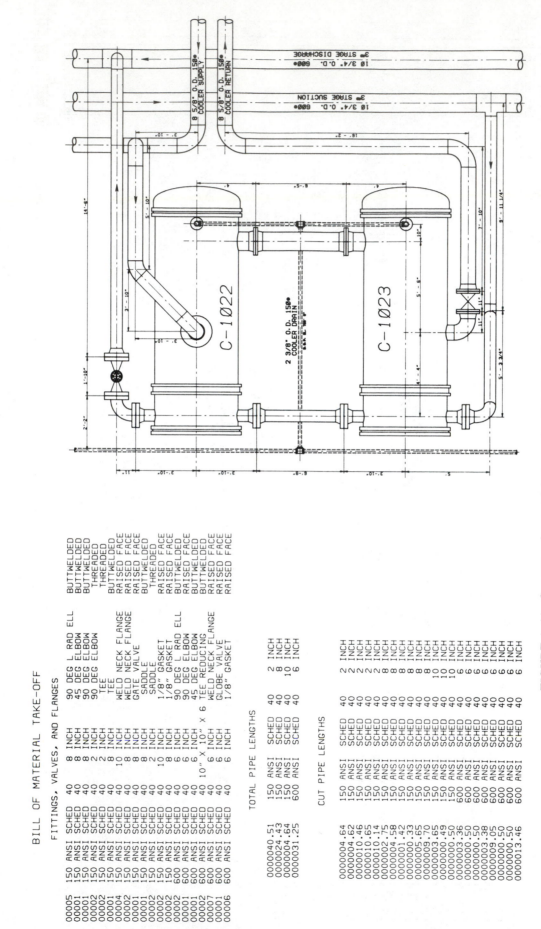

FIGURE 4-41 Computer-drawn piping sample. (Courtesy of Auto-trol Technology Corporation.)

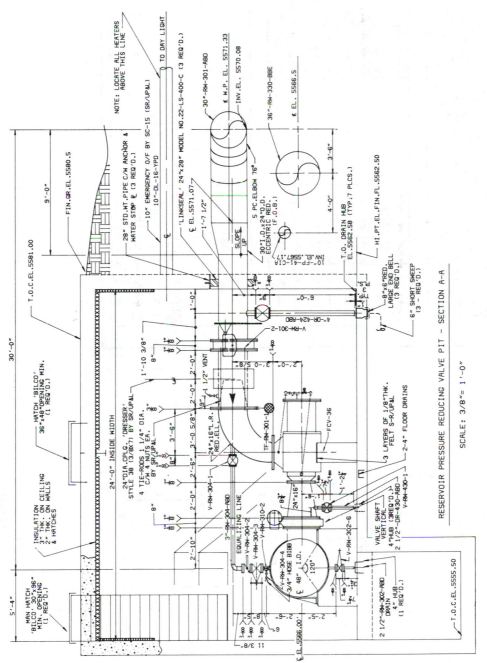

FIGURE 4-42 Computer-drawn piping sample. (Courtesy of Auto-trol Technology Corporation.)

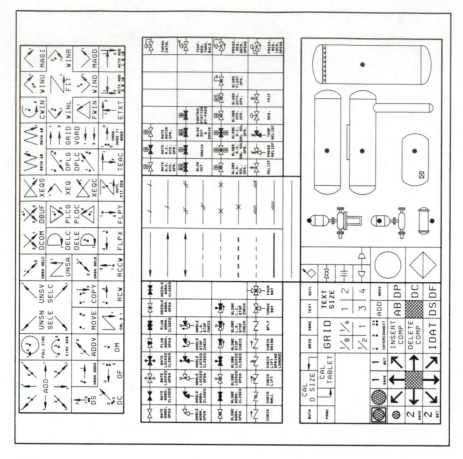

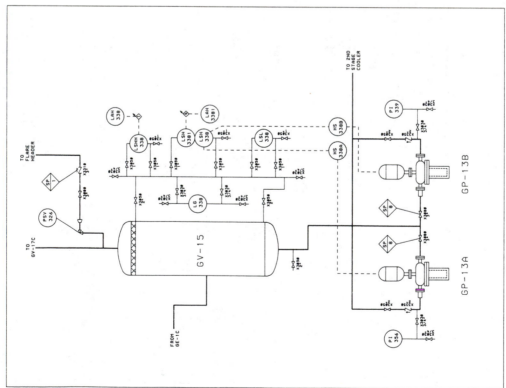

FIGURE 4-43 Computer-drawn piping sample. (Courtesy of Applicon Incorporated.)

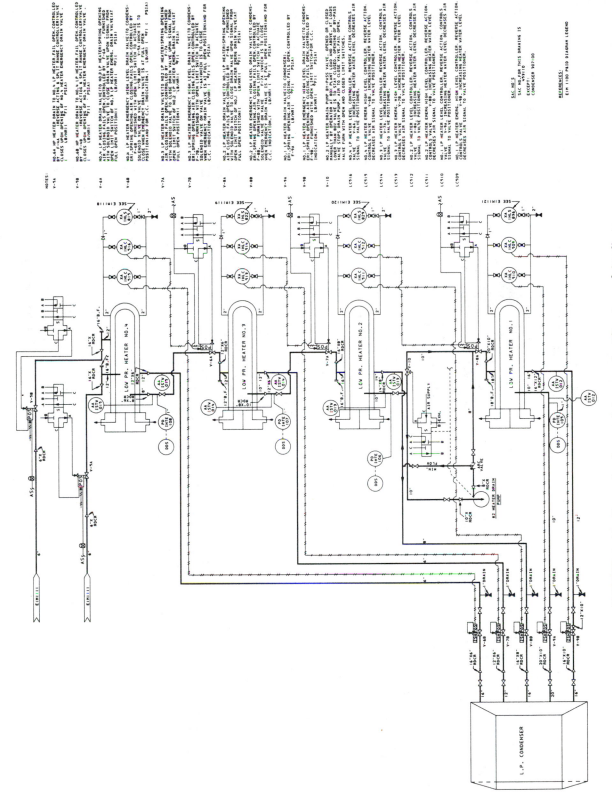

FIGURE 4-44 Computer-drawn piping sample. (Courtesy of Applicon Incorporated.)

103

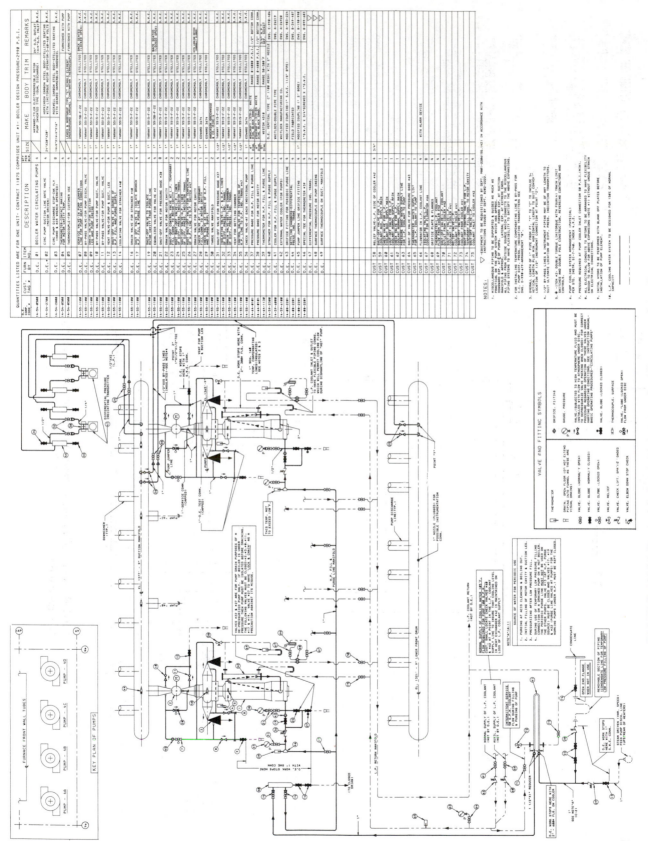

FIGURE 4-45 Computer-drawn piping sample. (Courtesy of Applicon Incorporated.)

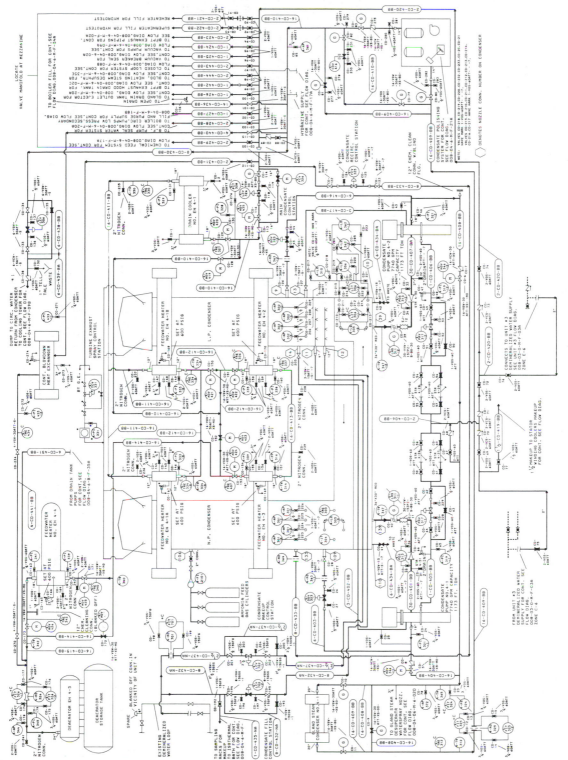

FIGURE 4-46 Computer-drawn piping sample. (Courtesy of Applicon Incorporated.)

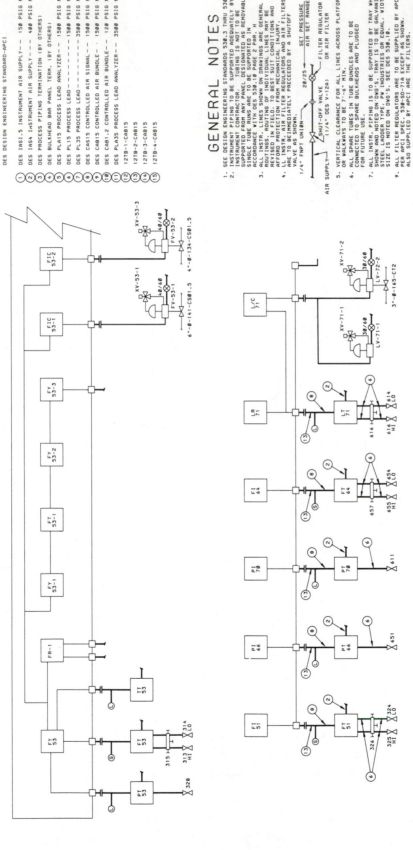

FIGURE 4-47 Computer-drawn piping sample. (Courtesy of Applicon Incorporated.)

GENERAL NOTES

1. SEE DESIGN ENGINEERING STANDARDS 530.3 THRU 530.10

2. INSTRUMENT PIPING TO BE SUPPORTED ADEQUATELY BY INSTRUMENT CONTRACTOR. TUBING IS NOT TO BE SUPPORTED FROM ANY PANEL DESIGNATED AS REMOVABLE. SINGLE TUBE RUNS ARE TO BE SUPPORTED IN ACCORDANCE WITH DES 530.10 PAGE 2 PAR. H

3. ALL INSTR. LINES SHOWN ON DRAWINGS ARE GENERAL ROUTINGS. ROUTING OF INDIVIDUAL LINES MAY BE REVISED ACCORDING TO BEST SUIT CONDITIONS AND AFFORD PROTECTION FROM MECHANICAL INJURY.

4. LL INSTR. AIR FILTER REGULATORS AND AIR FILTERS ARE TO BEIMMEDIATELY PRECEEDED BY A SHUTOFF VALVE AS SHOWN.

5. VERTICAL CLEARANCE FOR ALL LINES ACROSS PLATFORMS OR WALKWAYS TO BE 7'-6" MIN.

6. ALL SPARE TUBES IN TUBE BUNDLES ARE TO BE CONNECTED TO SPARE BULKHEADS AND PLUGGED FOR FUTURE USE.

7. ALL INSTR. PIPING IS TO BE SUPPORTED BY TRAY WHERE SHOWN AND NOTED ON DWG'S. TRAY IS TO BE GALVANIZED STEEL LADDER TYPE, PW INDUSTRIES OR EQUAL. WIDTH SIZE IS NOTED ON DWG'S. SEE DES 530.10.

8. ALL FILTER REGULATORS ARE TO BE SUPPLIED BY APCI PER APCI SPEC. 530-SD-71A EXCEPT AS SHOWN. ALSO SUPPLIED BY APCI ARE THE FILTERS.

10. FOR TUBE BUNDLE TAB. SEE DWG. NO. 5-3204-0005D.

DES DESIGN ENGINEERING STANDARD-APCI

1. DES IAS1.5 INSTRUMENT AIR SUPPLY ——— 150 PSIG MAX.
2. DES IAS4 INSTRUMENT AIR SUPPLY ——— 400 PSIG MAX.
3. DES PROCESS PIPING TERMINATION (BY OTHERS)
4. DES BULKHEAD BAR PANEL TERM. (BY OTHERS)
5. DES PLA15 PROCESS LEAD ANALYZER ——— 1500 PSIG MAX.
6. DES PL15 PROCESS LEAD ——— 1500 PSIG MAX.
7. DES PL35 PROCESS LEAD ——— 3500 PSIG MAX.
8. DES CAS15 CONTROLLED AIR SIGNAL ——— 1500 PSIG MAX.
9. DES CAB15 CONTROLLED AIR BUNDLE ——— 1500 PSIG MAX.
10. DES CAB1.2 CONTROLLED AIR BUNDLE ——— 120 PSIG MAX.
11. DES PLA35 PROCESS LEAD ANALYZER ——— 3500 PSIG MAX.
12. 12TB-1-CAB15
13. 12TB-2-CAB15
14. 12TB-3-CAB15
15. 12TB-4-CAB15

REFERENCE DRAWINGS

EQUIPMENT ARRANGEMENT PLAN
EQUIP. AND PIPING ARRGT. PLAN COMPRESSOR AREA
EQUIP. AND PIPING ARRGT. PLAN STOR. AND VAPORIZER AREA
EQUIP. AND PIPING ARRGT. PLAN COLD BOX AND AUX. SKID AREA
EQUIP. AND PIPING ARRGT. PLAN AFTER COOLER AREA
EQUIP. AND PIPING ARRGT. SECTIONS AND DETAIL STOR. AND VAPORIZER AREA
EQUIP. AND PIPING ARRGT. SECTION COLD BOX AREA
EQUIP. AND PIPING ARRGT. SECTION COLD BOX AND AUX. SKID AREA
EQUIP. AND PIPING SECTIONS COLD BOX AREA
EQUIP. AND PIPING ARRGT. SECTIONS DISP. VAPORIZER AND Ø1.14 SEPARATOR AREA
EQUIP. AND PIPING ARRGT. COMPRESSOR AREA
INSTRUMENT PIPING SCHEMATIC COLD BOX

5-3204-6200E
5-3204-6201D
5-3204-6202D
5-3204-6203D
5-3204-6204D
5-3204-6205D
5-3204-6206D
5-3204-6208D
5-3204-6209D
5-3204-6210D
5-3204-6211D
5-3204-6212D
3009777D SH. 2 OF 2

CONTRACT DRAWINGS

INSTRUMENT SCHEMATICS
INSTRUMENT PIPING PLAN STORAGE AND VAPORIZER AREA
INSTRUMENT PIPING PLAN AFTER COOLER AREA
INSTRUMENT PIPING PLAN COMPRESSOR AREA
INSTRUMENT PIPING PLAN AND TUBE BUNDLE TABULATION
INSTRUMENT COLD BOX AND AUX. SKID AREA
INSTRUMENT PIPING SECTIONS COLD BOX AREA
INSTRUMENT PIPING SECTION AND DETAILS COLD BOX AREA
VALVE SUMMARY
INSTRUMENT SUMMARY
INSTRUMENT SUMMARY - INSTALLED BY LEGEND

5-3204-0001D
5-3204-0002D
5-3204-0003D
5-3204-0004D
5-3204-0005D
5-3204-0006D
5-3204-0007D
5-3204-55.10-030
5-3204-1200-01A
530-SD-50A

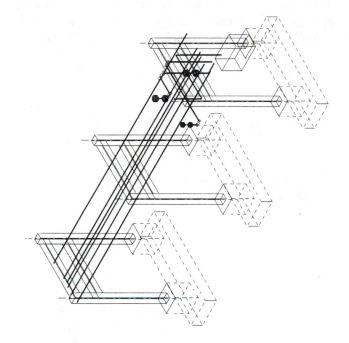

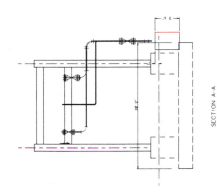

SECTION A-A

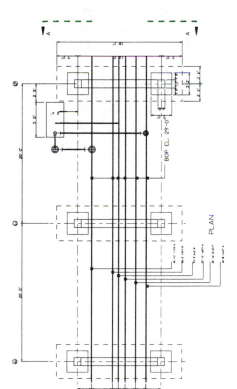

PLAN

BOP EL. 29'-0"

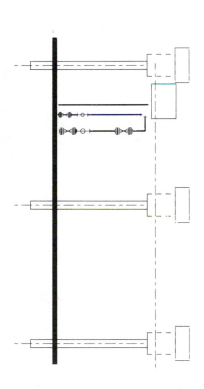

FIGURE 4-48 Computer-drawn piping sample. (Courtesy of Applicon Incorporated.)

107

Once a pictorial drawing has been entered into the system, it can be called up, displayed on the CRT screen, and rotated to produce an endless number of different views. Rather than starting over from scratch the computer drafting technician simply presses the "rotate" button and then the "plot" button. While the plotter is drawing one view, the drafter can be rotating the picture on the CRT screen for the next view. Figures 4–49 through 4–55 present samples of pictorial drawings done on a computer drafting system.

FIGURE 4–49 Computer-drawn pictoral sample. (Courtesy of Auto-trol Technology Corporation.)

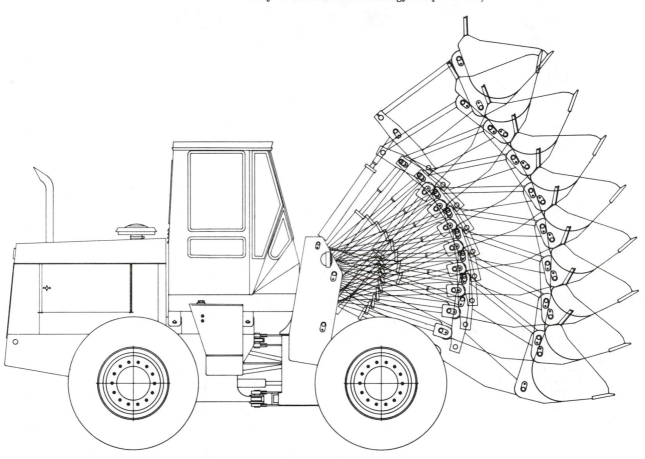

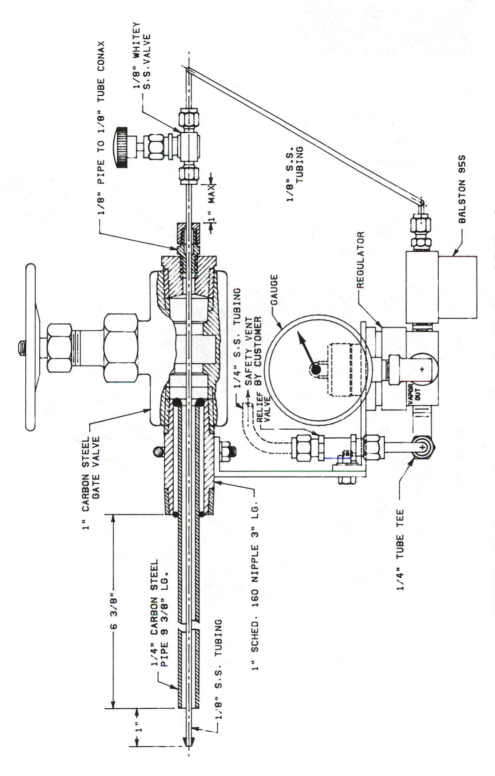

FIGURE 4-50 Computer-drawn pictorial sample. (Courtesy of Phillips Petroleum Company.)

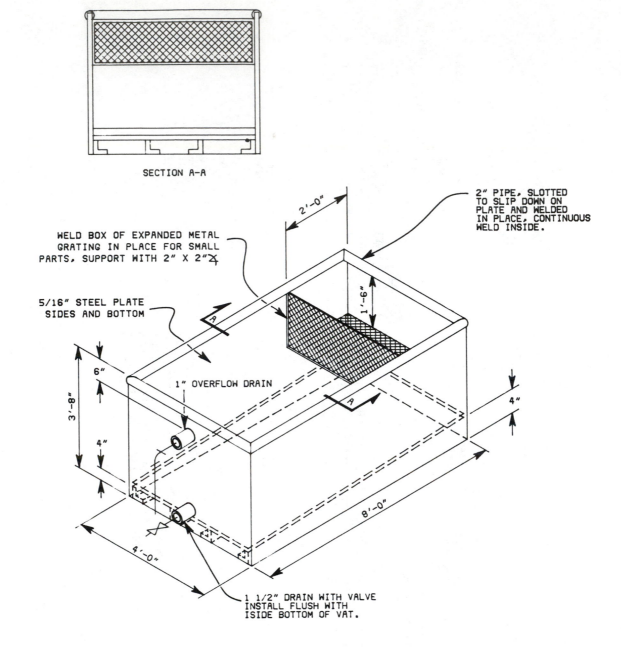

SECTION A-A

2" PIPE, SLOTTED TO SLIP DOWN ON PLATE AND WELDED IN PLACE, CONTINUOUS WELD INSIDE.

WELD BOX OF EXPANDED METAL GRATING IN PLACE FOR SMALL PARTS, SUPPORT WITH 2" X 2"

5/16" STEEL PLATE SIDES AND BOTTOM

2'-0"

1'-9"

6"

3'-8"

4"

4"

1" OVERFLOW DRAIN

8'-0"

4'-0"

1 1/2" DRAIN WITH VALVE INSTALL FLUSH WITH ISIDE BOTTOM OF VAT.

FIGURE 4-51 Computer-drawn pictorial sample. (Courtesy of Phillips Petroleum.)

110

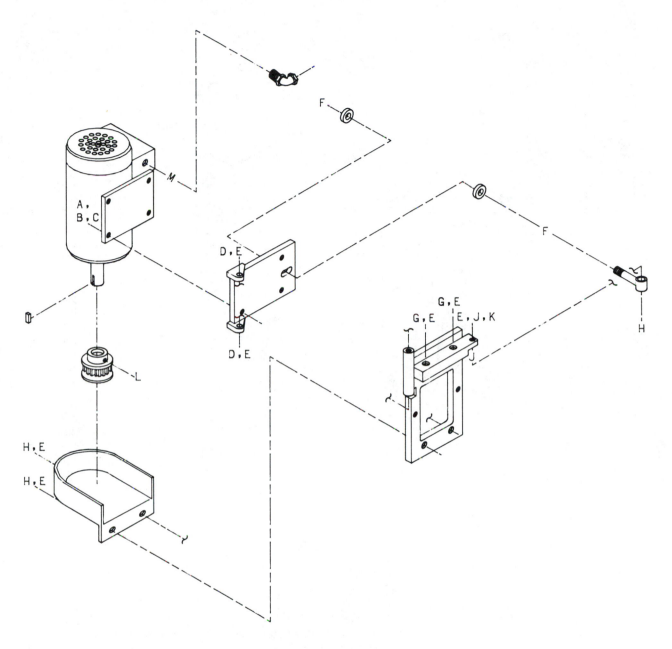

FIGURE 4-52 Computer-drawn pictorial sample. (Courtesy of Phillips Petroleum.)

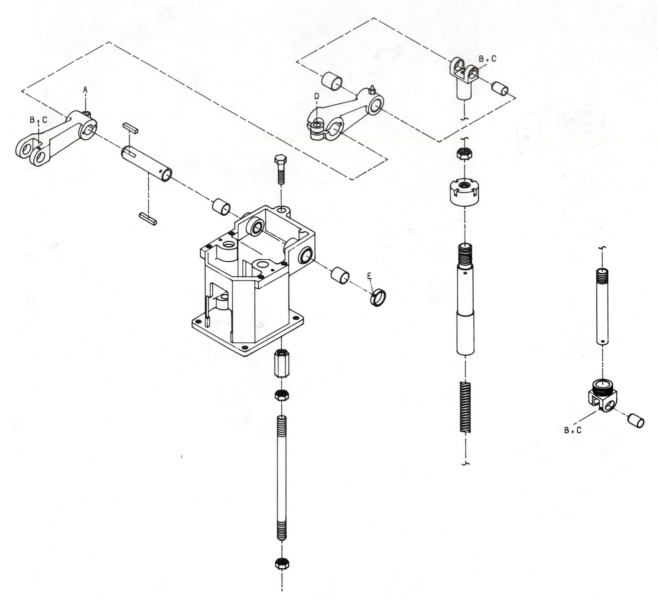

FIGURE 4-53 Computer-drawn pictorial sample. (Courtesy of Phillips Petroleum.)

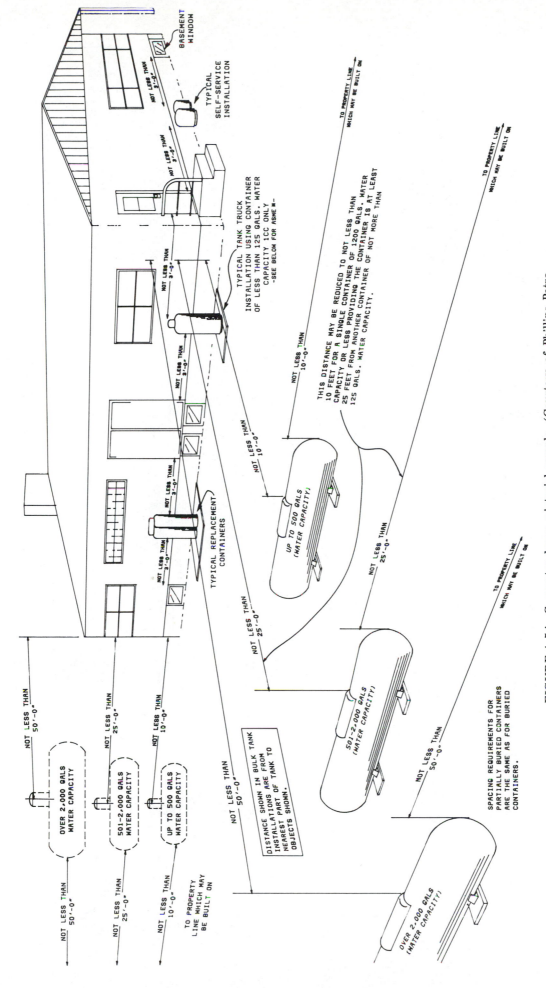

FIGURE 4-54 Computer-drawn pictorial sample. (Courtesy of Phillips Petroleum Company.)

113

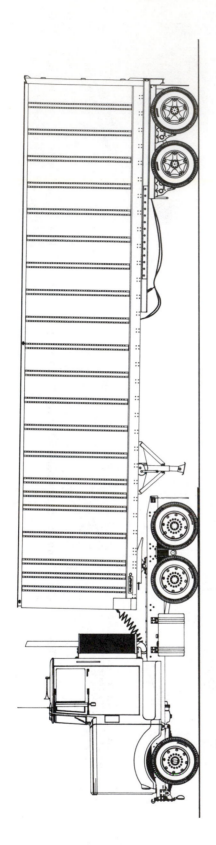

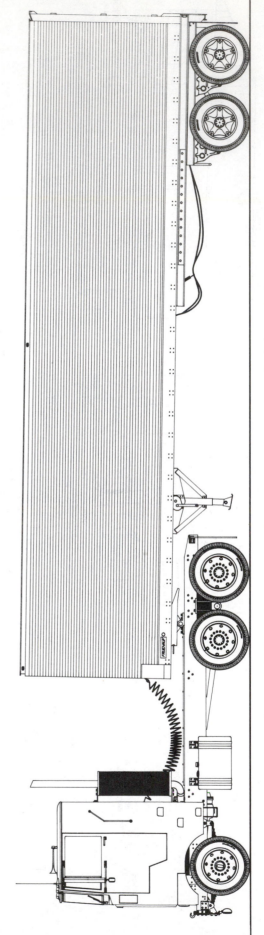

FIGURE 4-55 Computer-drawn pictorial sample. (Courtesy of Freuhauf Corporation.)

**SUMMARY
AND REVIEW**

- Interest in computer-aided drafting began to develop on a large scale in the early 1970s. By 1990, computer-aided drafting will probably be the norm even in smaller companies.

- The computer can be used not only in producing drawings, but also in compiling parts lists and bills of material, developing schedules, and in performing mathematical computations.

- Human beings' inherent slowness and inaccuracy in performing manual drafting tasks such as lettering, linework, and scalework, coupled with ever-increasing demands for higher levels of productivity, led to the wide-scale development of computer-aided drafting.

- Computer-aided drafting is not a new drafting field which has sprung up. Rather, it is a way of doing drafting which transcends all drafting fields.

- Drafting began to flourish as an occupation when industry converted to mass production methods.

- Computer-aided drafting is the latest in a long line of technological advances, such as drafting machines, templates, adjustable triangles, and reprographics, which have been designed to make the drafter more productive.

- The single most important benefit of computer-aided drafting is increased productivity.

- In most drafting applications, computer-aided drafting is from 5 to 20 times faster than manual techniques.

- In addition to producing drawings, computer-aided drafting systems can be used to perform engineering and design calculations, for cost estimation and material take-offs, for project scheduling, and for storage of drawings.

- Computer-aided drafting will not eliminate the need for drafters. Rather, it will allow drafters to do their jobs faster and better.

- The computer drafting technician needs the same basic drafting skills as the manual drafter as well as some new skills, such as a basic knowledge of computers, computer math skills, familiarity with a programming language, digitizing skills, and keyboard manipulation skills.

- Drafters do not normally develop the software for computer-aided drafting systems.

- Compared with manually prepared drawings, computer-produced drawings are superior in quality of lettering, scaling accuracy, and overall appearance.

- Computer-aided drafting can be done in all drafting fields. The most promising developments have been in the areas of architectural, civil, electronics, mechanical, piping, and pictorial drafting.

SELF-TEST   Directions

Complete the self-test without referring to the chapter. Once all questions have been answered, check them by referring to the appropriate sections of the chapter. Correct all questions answered incorrectly before proceeding to the next chapter.

1. Indicate whether each of the following statements is true or false.
   a. Computer-aided drafting is a new drafting field to be added to the list of drafting fields already in existence.
   b. Drafting began to flourish as an occupation when industry converted to mass production techniques.
   c. Computer-aided drafting is the latest in a long line of technological advances which have been designed to make the drafter more productive.
   d. Computer-aided drafting is really only about twice as fast as manual drafting in most applications.
   e. Drafters do not normally develop the software for computer-aided drafting systems.

2. Name three things besides producing drawings that computer-aided drafting systems can be used to do.

3. What is the single most important benefit of computer-aided drafting?

4. List four skills beyond the basic drafting skills which are needed by computer drafting technicians.

5. When is it expected that computer-aided drafting systems will be in wide-scale use even among smaller companies employing a drafting force?

6. What led to the eventual development and acceptance of computer-aided drafting?

7. Expound on the following statement: "Computer-aided drafting will not eliminate the need for drafters."

8. Explain how computer-aided drafting is being used in the following drafting fields: architectural; electronics.

5

COMPUTER-AIDED
DRAFTING SYSTEMS

OBJECTIVES Upon completion of this chapter, you will be able to:

1. List the three components of a computer-aided drafting system.
2. Explain the functions of each piece of equipment in a typical computer-aided drafting hardware configuration.
3. Explain the different types of software packages used in computer-aided drafting systems.
4. Write a job description for "computer-aided drafting technician" and for "computer-aided drafting system operator."

Although manufacturers of computer-aided drafting hardware advertise their products as computer-aided drafting systems, their products are really only part of a system, the hardware. A complete computer-aided drafting system consists of three components: the hardware, the software, and the users (Figure 5–1).

The hardware in a computer-aided drafting system can range from a small configuration consisting of only a few items to a large configuration with numerous items of hardware and multiple applications potential. A small hardware configuration made up of two CRT workstations, a processing unit, and a printer is shown in Figure 5–2. This configuration would be used primarily for alphanumeric (num-

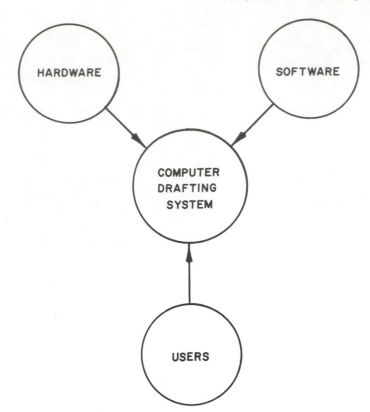

FIGURE 5-1   Computer-aided drafting system.

FIGURE 5-2   Computer-aided drafting system hardware. (Courtesy of WANG Laboratories, Inc.)

bers, letters, and characters that can be entered from a keyboard) input and output. A limited graphic capability (lines, points, planes, arcs, circles, etc.), is available on the screen of the CRTs. Figure 5-3 shows an example of a medium-sized hardware configuration with both keyboard and digitizing capabilities. This configuration could handle both alphanumeric and graphic input and output.

FIGURE 5-3 Computer-aided drafting system hardware. (Courtesy of ComputerVision.)

Each individual piece of equipment in a computer-aided drafting system hardware configuration serves a special purpose. Students of computer-aided drafting should be familiar with all the various pieces of hardware that might be found in a typical hardware configuration.

A TYPICAL HARDWARE CONFIGURATION

Companies that employ drafters differ in many ways. There are architectural companies, engineering companies, manufacturing companies, processing companies, and even retailing companies. There are large companies and small companies, companies which do a great deal of drafting and those which do very little. There are those which do engineering drawings and those which do shop drawings. There are those which do pictorial drawings and those which do a variety of different types of drawings.

Obviously, companies that employ a drafting force have a variety of needs in terms of drafting. Therefore, the size and type of computer-aided drafting systems used by different companies will vary as much as the companies themselves. To gain a thorough understanding of computer-aided drafting system hardware configurations and the various pieces of hardware that make them up, it is necessary to study a typical configuration which contains the most commonly used hardware items.

A typical hardware configuration would contain a CRT workstation, a digitizing unit, a plotter, a processing unit, a printer, and a hard-copy unit (Figure 5-4).

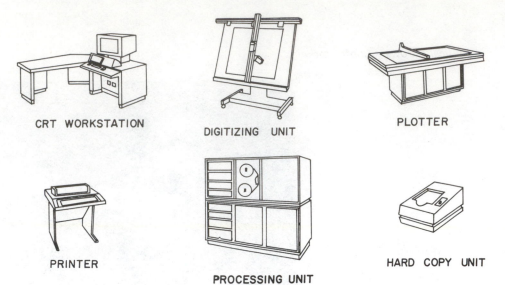

CRT WORKSTATION

DIGITIZING UNIT

PLOTTER

PRINTER

PROCESSING UNIT

HARD COPY UNIT

FIGURE 5-4   Typical computer-aided drafting configuration.

The CRT Workstation

The CRT workstation is the primary input device in a computer-aided drafting system. It can also be an output device for calling up information and displaying it on the CRT screen. The CRT workstation consists of a CRT screen for visual displays of both alphanumeric and graphic data, a keyboard for alphanumeric and character input, and thumb wheels for entering horizontal and vertical lines.

CRT workstations manufactured by different suppliers will have variations in design and appearance. However, most will contain the components listed above. Many will also have an interactive graphics tablet and an electronic pen for entering graphic data into the system. Figures 5-5 and 5-6 present examples of CRT workstations from two different hardware manufacturers.

FIGURE 5-5   CRT workstation. (Courtesy of Tektronix, Inc.)

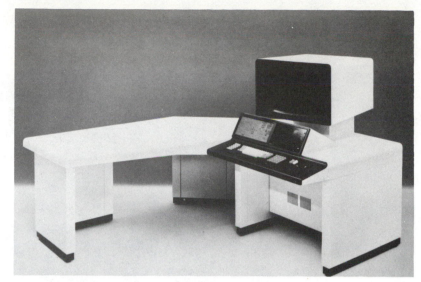

FIGURE 5-6 CRT workstation. (Courtesy of Auto-trol Technology Corporation.)

The Digitizing Unit

Computers operate on electrical impulses known as binary signals. For this reason, all data entered into a computer must be in digital form. With alphanumeric data this is simple and direct because numbers can easily be represented by binary signals or digits. However, the same is not true of graphic data.

Lines, points, planes, arcs, circles, and all the various other geometric configurations that make up the graphic language of drafting present a problem for the computer. Since they are graphic rather than digital, the computer cannot handle them. Therefore, to input graphic data into a computer requires an intermediate step known as digitizing.

Digitizing is the process through which graphic data are converted into digits or binary form so that the computer can accept and process them. The digitizing process is similar to tracing and can be accomplished using an electronic pen or cursor and digitizing tablet. Digitizing units range in size from small tablets (Figure 5-7) to large tables (Figure 5-8).

FIGURE 5-7 Digitizing tablet. (Courtesy of ComputerVision.)

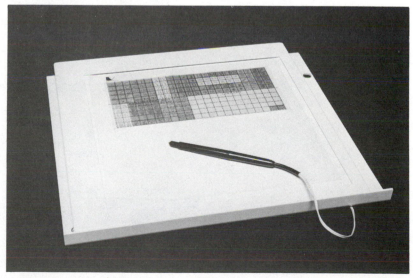

FIGURE 5-8 Digitizing unit. (Courtesy of ComputerVision.)

The Plotter

In the preceding section it was explained how graphic data must be converted to digital form in order to be accepted and processed by the computer. This is because computers operate on binary signals. However, human beings do not. Human beings need alphanumeric, character, and graphic representations of data. Therefore, in order for computer data to be used by human beings, the process explained above must be reversed. Graphic data are converted from digital representation in the computer back to graphic form by a plotter.

By commanding the plotter to plot a series of X-Y coordinates, the computer actually constructs drawings. The same types of drafting media used in manual drafting (ink, tracing vellum, polyester films, etc.), can be used on plotters. A plotter resembles an ultramodern drafting table with a drafting machine but no drafter. The drafting machine is moved electronically and can contain a number of different sizes of pens and colors of ink, all of which may be used simultaneously. Figures 5-9 and 5-10 present examples of plotters.

FIGURE 5-9 Flatbed plotter. (Courtesy of Tektronix, Inc.)

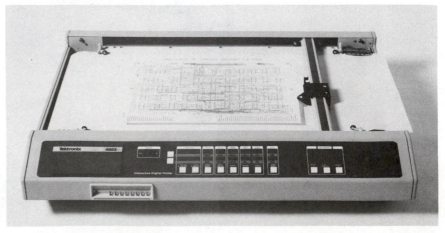

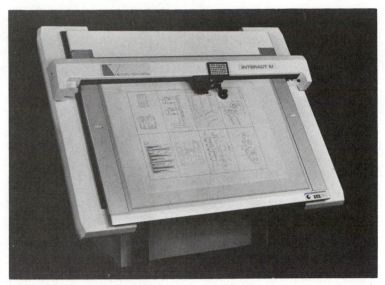

FIGURE 5-10   Flatbed plotter. (Courtesy of ComputerVision.)

The Processing Unit

Although the configurations of various computer-aided drafting systems will differ in makeup, the one hardware item that they all have in common is the processing unit. The processing unit is the "brain" or CPU of the computer-aided drafting system. Its physical construction is very similar to the CPUs used in business, health, and military applications in that it has a control section and an arithmetic section. However, in addition, it has special features designed in for processing of graphic data. This is the major difference between a processing unit for a computer-aided drafting system and that for a business, health, or military computer system.

FIGURE 5-11   Processing unit for a computer-aided drafting system. (Courtesy of Auto-trol Technology Corporation.)

Figure 5–11 contains an example of a processing unit used in a computer-aided drafting system. Just as in all computer systems, the memory capability of the processing unit for a computer-aided drafting system may be expanded with the addition of tape drives or disk drives (Figures 5–12 and 5–13).

FIGURE 5-12   Tape drive. (Courtesy of ComputerVision.)

FIGURE 5-13   Disk drive. (Courtesy of ComputerVision.)

The Printer

Printed matter such as program documentation, bills of material, parts lists, schedules, supply inventories, and so forth are all integral parts of the drafting department work load in most companies. In a computer-aided drafting system, printed materials can be generated efficiently and rapidly on a piece of hardware called a printer.

There are impact printers and matrix printers. *Impact* printers create alphanumeric characters in much the same way as a typewriter. *Matrix* printers create characters through a series of small dots arranged in a matrix in such a way as to form the desired letter or numeral.

Some printers are interfaced with the CRT workstation and input originates on the workstation keyboard. Other printers are freestanding and have their own keyboards. These printers may also be interfaced with the CRT workstation and operated from either location.

Printers are rated according to the quality of the characters they imprint, the number of characters per second they are capable of printing, the number of characters per line they can print, and the number of lines to the vertical inch that they can print. A fast printer can print almost 200 characters per second for certain types of output. A character and line capacity common to most printers used in computer-aided drafting systems would be approximately 130 characters per line and six lines to the vertical inch. There are numerous styles and types of printers on the market. Figures 5–14 through 5–18 present examples of printers.

FIGURE 5–14 Printer. (Courtesy of ComputerVision.)

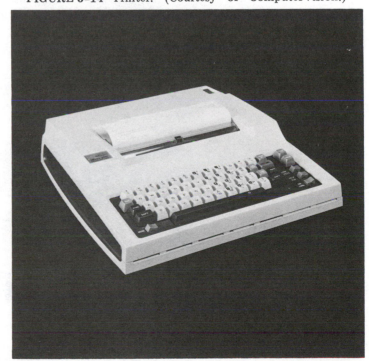

FIGURE 5-15 Line printer. (Courtesy of Radio Shack, a Division of Tandy Corporation.)

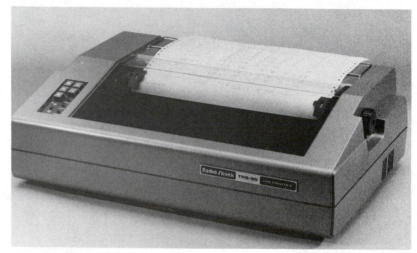

FIGURE 5-16 Line printer. (Courtesy of Radio Shack, a Division of Tandy Corporation.)

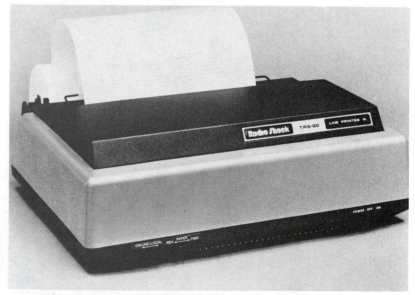

FIGURE 5-17 Line printer. (Courtesy of Radio Shack, a Division of Tandy Corporation.)

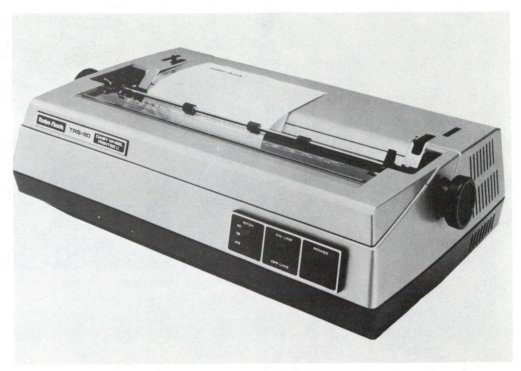

FIGURE 5–18 Daisywheel printer. (Courtesy of Radio Shack, a Division of Tandy Corporation.)

The Hard-Copy Unit

On occasion, data represented on the CRT workstation screen will need to be preserved. At other times, a designer will want to check a drawing that is displayed on the CRT screen before it is plotted. When these and similar situations arise, the hard-copy unit is used. A hard-copy unit is a hardware item that can provide a high-quality photocopy of data, both graphic and alphanumeric, which appear on the CRT workstation screen.

A hard-copy unit can be a very valuable addition to a computer aided drafting system. Copies of data displayed on the CRT screen are of high quality, small enough to fit into a normal size file folder, made on paper that readily accepts pencil or pen notations, and take only about 10 to 20 seconds to develop.

There are hundreds of uses for a hard-copy unit in a computer-aided drafting system. An example of how a hard-copy unit is commonly used would be the following. A designer gives a computer-aided drafting technician a rough sketch of a mechanical part. The drafter is to digitize the sketch, add dimensions, add the necessary notation, and plot a completed working drawing of the part. However, to avoid mistakes, the designer asks to see a hard copy of the drawing before it is plotted. The hard-copy unit can also be used to document preliminary stages in the development of a product by providing copies of drawings in each stage of development. Figure 5–19 contains an example of a hard-copy unit for a computer-aided drafting system.

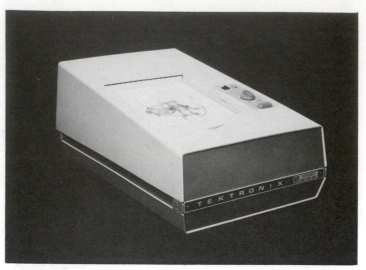

FIGURE 5-19   Hard-copy unit. (Courtesy of Tektronix, Inc.)

SOFTWARE   The key to the flexibility of a computer-aided drafting system is the software available for the system. As has already been discussed, computer drafting technicians do not normally develop the software for a computer-aided drafting system, although they do sometimes participate in the development of user software. In spite of this, they need to be familiar with the various types of software which are an integral part of any computer-aided drafting system.

Software for a computer-aided drafting system falls into one of four categories: operational software, graphics software, applications software, and user software (Figure 5-20).

Operational software makes possible the general operation of a computer-aided drafting system. This includes such tasks as memory allocation, scheduling of the processing unit, driving of input/output devices, arranging of priorities of operations, and interrupting of operations.

Graphics software is designed especially to allow the computer to deal with graphic data. This includes the ability to enter, manipulate, edit, revise, correct, and store two- and three-dimensional data such as points, lines, planes, arcs, and circles.

Applications software provides for the performance of drafting tasks within specific drafting fields, such as architectural, civil, electronics, mechanical, piping, and pictorial drafting. It also allows for specific tasks within each of these drafting fields, such as drawing engineering, layout, erection, or shop drawings.

User software is that which is developed by the computer-aided drafting system user at the workplace for applications that are specific to the user's company. User software is task oriented and frequently consists of such things as special-purpose computer-aided drafting templates known as *menus*, or special styles of lettering fonts. A menu is the electronic equivalent of a template. It resembles a large rectangular card which contains symbols or geometric shapes that are frequently used in a given drafting setting. By using the

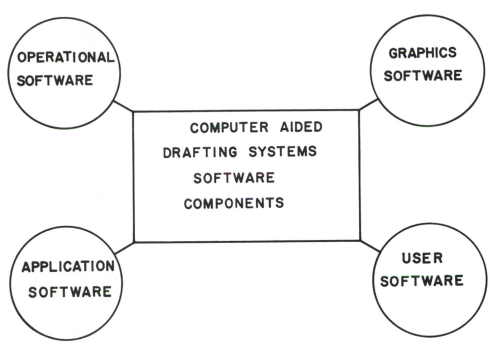

FIGURE 5-20 Computer-aided drafting software types.

menu in conjunction with a digitizing implement such as an electronic pen or a cursor, the drafter is able to enter frequently used symbols or geometric shapes by simply pressing a button.

THE USER A user is any person who uses a computer-aided drafting system to perform drafting tasks. Users may be engineers, designers, drafters, or computer-aided drafting system operators. This textbook is for people who are or hope to be either computer-aided drafting technicians or computer-aided drafting system operators.

The Computer-Aided Drafting Technician

A computer-aided drafting technician is a drafter in a particular drafting field who has learned to perform all, or more realistically most, of his or her drafting tasks on a computer-aided drafting system. The typical computer-aided drafting technician would be a person who is well experienced in a given drafting field, say architectural or electronics drafting, who learns the automated methods for performing tasks he or she has historically done manually.

Computer-aided drafting technicians may be found in all drafting fields. They still need all the traditional knowledge and skills that are intrinsic to their particular drafting field. However, in addition, they must acquire new knowledge and skills. Computer-aided drafting technicians must learn general computer knowledge, programming language familiarity, computer-related math, and computer-aided drafting system operational skills such as digitizing and keyboard use. Figure 5-21 presents a checklist of skills needed by the computer-aided drafting technician.

X	Neat, fast, freehand lettering
X	Neat, fast linework skills
X	Scalework skills
X	Dimensioning skills
X	Orthographic projection skills
X	Axonometric projection skills
X	Oblique drawing skills
X	Sectioning skills
X	Three-dimensional thinking skills
X	Visualization skills
X	Digitizing skills
X	Keyboard skills
X	Electronic pen skills
X	General computer knowledge
X	Computer math skills
X	Basic knowledge of a programming language
X	Menu development skills
X	Menu-use skills
X	Thorough knowledge of the drafting field being practiced

FIGURE 5-21 Computer-aided drafting user skills checklist.

The Computer-Aided Drafting System Operator

A computer-aided drafting system operator is a person who has system operating skills but may have little or no background in the particular drafting field being practiced. For example: A large manufacturing firm has converted to automated drafting and has installed a complete computer-aided drafting system. It has hired people skilled in the operation of the system hardware. However, these people know nothing about manufacturing processes, surface treatment of metals, material properties, threaded fasteners, jigs and fixtures, gears and cams, drafting standards, or working drawings. They simply take the raw data provided by designers or drafters and enter it into the system, digitize data, key in data, call up stored data, print data, and plot data.

Operators are skilled workers, but only in the computer-aided drafting system operational area. They are not skilled drafters. The distinction between a computer-aided drafting technician and an operator is much the same as the distinction between a machinist and a machine operator. It is in the area of scope of knowledge and skills.

An operator's skills include such things as digitizing skills, keyboard skills, editing skills, plotting skills, and other operational skills. Although many companies who convert to computer-aided drafting do employ computer-aided drafting system operators, problems can arise when operators are entering data with which they are not familiar. Time can be saved when the computer-aided drafting system user is also well trained in the drafting field being practiced. Therefore, the technician position is usually considered the higher of the two.

Whether a person works as a technician or an operator in using a computer-aided drafting system, he or she will perform such tasks as digitizing of graphic data (Figure 5-22), entering of alphanumeric data through a keyboard (Figure 5-23), manipulating data displayed on the CRT workstation screen (Figure 5-24), and calling up and plotting of data to create drawings (Figure 5-25).

FIGURE 5-22   Entering data into the system. (Courtesy of The Rust Engineering Company.)

FIGURE 5-23   Entering alphanumeric data with keyboard. (Courtesy of The Rust Engineering Company.)

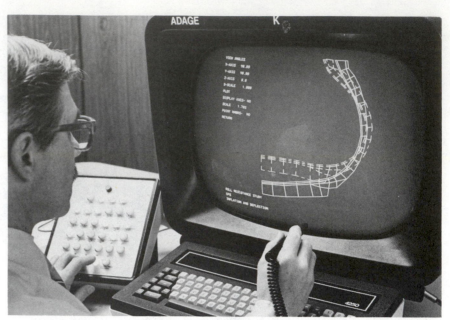

FIGURE 5-24 Manipulating displayed data. (Courtesy of Goodyear Tire and Rubber Company.)

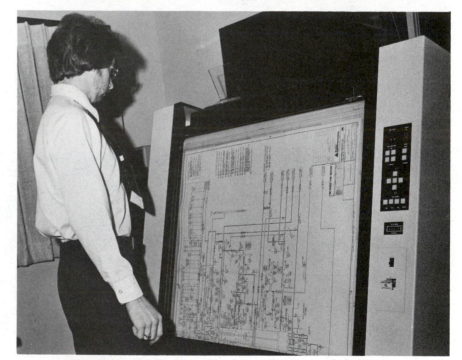

FIGURE 5-25 Plotting drawings. (Courtesy of the Rust Engineering Company.)

SUMMARY AND REVIEW

- A complete computer-aided drafting system consists of three components: the hardware, the software, and the users.

- A typical computer-aided drafting system hardware configuration would contain: a CRT workstation, a digitizing unit, a plotter, a processing unit, a printer, and a hard-copy unit.

- The CRT workstation is the primary input device of the computer-aided drafting system. It consists of a CRT screen, a keyboard, thumbwheels, and an interactive graphics tablet.

- The digitizing unit is used for converting graphic data into digital data so that the computer can accept and process it.

- The plotter creates drawings by plotting a series of X-Y coordinates. It is the device within the computer-aided drafting system which converts digital data back into graphic form.

- The processing unit is the "brain" of the computer-aided drafting system. It has a control section and an arithmetic section like all CPUs, but it also has special design features for handling the various types of graphic data associated with drafting.

- Alphanumeric documentation for such things as reports, bills of material, parts lists, and so on, is generated on a printer. Printers are usually matrix printers or impact printers.

- An impact printer makes character impressions in much the same way as a typewriter. A matrix printer creates characters by arranging a series of small dots in a matrix to the desired configuration.

- The hard-copy unit is a piece of hardware that can provide high-quality photocopies of data displayed on the CRT screen in as little as 10 to 20 seconds.

- Computer-aided drafting system software falls into one of four categories: operational, graphic, application, and user.

- Operational software provides for memory allocation, scheduling of the processing unit, driving of input/output devices, arranging of operational priorities, and interrupting of operations.

- Graphics software allows computer-aided drafting systems to handle graphic data such as points, lines, planes, arcs, and circles in two or three dimensions.

- Applications software is that which is designed to allow the computer-aided drafting system to perform operations in specific drafting fields, such as architectural, civil, electronics, mechanical, piping, and pictorial drafting.

- User software is task oriented and provides for very specific operations which may be intrinsic to a given company or drafting setting. A special user-developed menu is an example of user software.

- The computer-aided drafting technician is a drafter who is skilled in both computer-aided drafting system operations and the specific drafting field being practiced by his or her company.

- The computer-aided drafting system operator is a skilled worker who has system operational skills but little or no background in the drafting field being practiced by his or her company.

● Since a computer-aided drafting technician is skilled at both system operation and drafting, he or she is considered in a higher position than a computer-aided drafting system operator.

SELF-TEST   Directions

Respond to the following questions without referring to the chapter. Once all questions have been answered, check your answers by referring to the appropriate section of the chapter. Correct all errors and reread any part of the chapter covering questions that you missed.

1. What is the purpose of the digitizing unit in a computer-aided drafting system?

2. What is the purpose of the plotter in a computer-aided drafting system?

3. Each of the statements below relates to one of the four basic types of computer-aided drafting system software. Read each statement and decide which of the four types of system software it pertains to: operational, graphics, applications, user.
   a. Provides for very specific tasks which are intrinsic to a given drafting setting.
   b. Provides for memory allocation in the processing unit.
   c. Allows the computer-aided drafting system to perform tasks in the area of mechanical drafting.
   d. Allows the computer-aided drafting system to handle graphic data.
   e. Provides for the driving of input/output devices within the system.

4. Define the phrase "computer-aided drafting technician."

5. Define the phrase "computer-aided drafting system operator."

6. Name two different types of printers used in computer-aided drafting systems.

7. Name the three components that make up a complete computer-aided drafting system.

8. List the components that would be included in a typical computer-aided drafting system hardware configuration.

9. Indicate whether each of the following statements is true or false.
   a. The CRT workstation is the primary input device in a computer-aided drafting system.
   b. The processing unit is the "brain" of a computer-aided drafting system.
   c. A hard-copy unit is used primarily as an input device in a computer-aided drafting system.

d. A line printer creates impressions by arranging small dots in a matrix.

e. A computer-aided drafting technician must have both drafting and system operation skills.

f. Alphanumeric data consist of such things as points, lines, planes, arcs, and circles.

g. The plotter converts digital data back into graphic form so that they can be used by human beings.

10. Explain the difference between a computer-aided drafting technician and a computer-aided drafting system operator.

6

DOING COMPUTER-AIDED DRAFTING

OBJECTIVES Upon completion of this chapter, you will be able to:

1. Explain the three basic operations in computer-aided drafting.

2. Explain such basic concepts of computer-aided drafting as plotting coordinates, resolution in plotting, accuracy, repeatability, plotting limitations, and paper sizes.

3. Demonstrate proficiency in performing (or explaining how to perform) such drafting tasks as lettering, linework, scalework, and dimensioning on a computer-aided drafting system.

4. Explain how such drafting processes as checking drawings, correcting drawings, and storing drawings are accomplished on a computer-aided drafting system.

OVERVIEW OF COMPUTER-AIDED DRAFTING TECHNIQUES Computer-aided drafting means exactly what the name implies — using the computer as an aid in facilitating the overall drafting process from creating original drawings, to checking and correcting drawings, to storing drawings. The computer, by itself, does not create, check, correct, or store drawings. These are all functions performed by drafters with the aid of computer drafting hardware and software.

In this chapter you will learn how to perform on a computer-aided drafting system all of the more common drafting tasks traditionally done manually. Information in this chapter will assist you in developing the actual skills necessary to become a computer-aided drafting technician.

Basic Operations

Computer-aided drafting involves three basic operations: input of data, manipulation of data, and output of data. For inputting and manipulating data, computer-aided drafting technicians use such tools as CRT keyboards, digitizing tablets, electronic pens, cursors, and menus (Figures 6-1 through 6-4).

FIGURE 6-1   Computer-aided drafting input device.

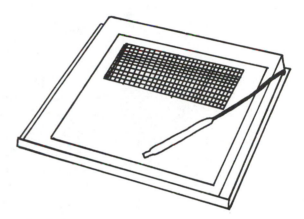

FIGURE 6-2   Computer-aided drafting input device.

FIGURE 6-3   Computer-aided drafting input device.

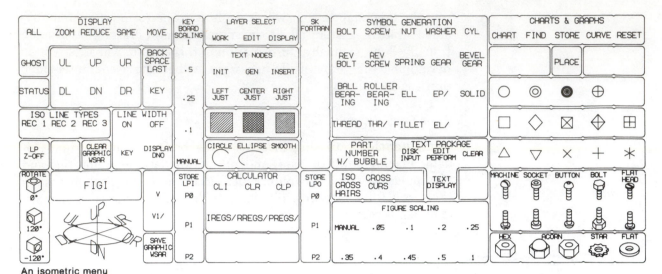

An isometric menu

FIGURE 6-4   Computer-aided drafting input device. (Courtesy of Auto-trol Technology Corporation.)

In the input phase, there are a number of different methods that can be used for getting data into the computer-aided drafting system. The most effective method of entering graphic data is the digitizing process. In this process, the sketch provided the drafter is taped to either a digitizing tablet or board and electronically traced using either a cursor or an electronic pen. In this way, graphical data such as lines, arcs, circles, and other geometric shapes are converted to electrical impulses.

A sketch is one of the most common starting points in both manual and computer-aided drafting. In manual drafting, the drafter starts with a sketch, straightens out all lines mechanically, adds the necessary dimensions and notations, and finally converts the sketch into a finished working drawing. The process is the same for computer-aided drafting, except that the computer will automatically straighten out "sketchy" lines as they are input through the digitizing process. Figures 6-5 and 6-6 illustrate this principle. Figure 6-5 presents a designer's sketch of a part to be machined. Notice

FIGURE 6-5   Designer's sketch.

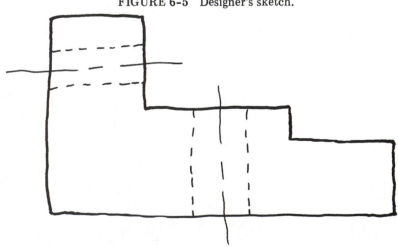

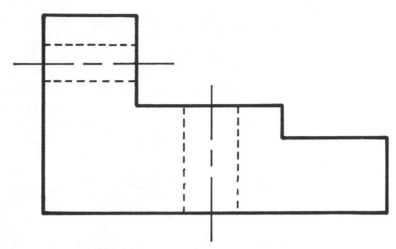

FIGURE 6-6 Computer-generated drawing of the sketch.

the "sketchy" nature of the lines. Figure 6-6 presents the computer-generated drawing of the same part. Notice that the computer has straightened out the lines. Digitizing gets the graphical data into the computer's memory. The next step involves calling the stored data up on the CRT screen where they will be displayed as a drawing, and performing any necessary manipulations (Figure 6-7).

Manipulating data means performing certain types of modifications to the drawing that is displayed on the CRT screen. The manipulation capability is one of the computer-aided drafting systems' most important advantages over manual drafting. Systems with this capa-

FIGURE 6-7 Performing drawing manipulations. (Courtesy of Applicon Incorporated.)

bility are able to "zoom in" for close-ups of a drawing, "zoom out" for a broader perspective, rotate drawings for viewing from different angles, and even mirror symmetrical drawings.

Once a drawing displayed on the CRT screen has been completed to the drafter's satisfaction and all desired manipulations have been made, it is time for the output phase. This is the step in which original drawings (or hard copies) of the graphical data displayed on the CRT screen are made (Figure 6–8).

FIGURE 6–8 Plotting original drawings. (Courtesy of The Rust Engineering Company.)

BASIC CONCEPTS OF COMPUTER-AIDED DRAFTING

Like manual drafting, computer-aided drafting involves lettering, linework, dimensioning, notation, symbol creation, drawing manipulation, crosshatching, and so on. How these drafting tasks are actually performed on a computer-aided drafting system is discussed later in this chapter. However, before attempting to learn how these tasks are performed using automated techniques, the student must first understand some basic concepts that are fundamental to computer-aided drafting. These include such things as coordinate systems, resolution, repeatability, accuracy, computer-aided drafting hardware limitations, and computer-aided drafting paper sizes.

Coordinate Systems

It has been learned that computers operate on electrical impulses and that graphical data must therefore be digitized before they can be accepted by the computer. It was also learned that the computer must convert these electrical impulses back into graphical form in order for them to be used by human beings. The computer accomplishes this conversion by plotting X and Y coordinates on a simulated Cartesian coordinate system, which is either the CRT screen or the surface of the system's plotter.

In a coordinate system, points are represented by X-Y coordinates (or X-Y-Z coordinates in the case of three-dimensional drawings). Lines are created by plotting the X-Y coordinates that represent the ends of the lines (Figure 6-9). The plotting surface of the computer-aided drafting system, whether it is a CRT screen or a plotter, is viewed as a Cartesian coordinate system, usually with its origins at the lower left-hand corner of the plotting surface (Figure 6-10).

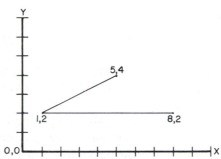

FIGURE 6-9   Plotting end points of a line.

FIGURE 6-10   Plotting on a Cartesian coordinate system.

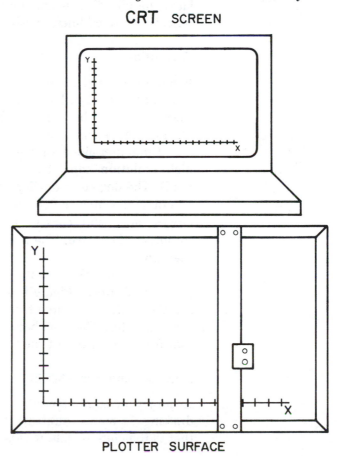

All geometric shapes, even circles, are formed by a series of lines. Since this is true, the computer is able to plot a graphic representation of any object that can be drawn manually. Figure 6–11 presents an example of a complete drawing with its coordinates and the direction of plotting shown. Notice that the first and last points of the plot are the same. This must be true in order for the plot to "close."

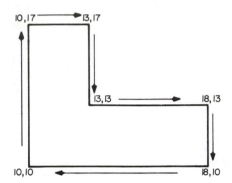

FIGURE 6-11 A drawing with its coordinates shown.

By computing coordinates, computer-aided drafting technicians can enter graphic data directly into the computer and have them displayed on the CRT screen by simply pressing buttons. However, calculating coordinates is a difficult, time-consuming process. Therefore, the most common practice is to sketch the desired object and then digitize it. When this is done, the computer automatically calculates the coordinates and plots the necessary points. With complex objects or curved lines, digitizing is the most practical method.

Resolution

It was mentioned above that all objects drawn by the computer are in reality a series of lines. This includes arcs, curves, and circles. How smooth a curved line will be when plotted on a computer-aided drafting system depends on the resolution capabilities of the system.

Computer-aided drafting systems are sometimes said to have high-resolution capabilities (good) or poor resolution capabilities (bad). The degree or quality of resolution has to do with the number of points per inch the computer plots in making the lines that form circles, arcs, and curves. The more points that are plotted, the smoother the curve. The fewer points that are plotted, the rougher the curve.

A computer's resolution capabilities are readily apparent in the plotting of circles. Figure 6–12 shows a computer-generated drawing for the trailer of a large truck. Notice the resolution capabilities of the computer. They can best be seen by closely examining the circles that form the wheels of the trailer.

Accuracy and Repeatability

Accuracy in computer-aided drafting is the same as it is in manual drafting. In manual drafting if the drafter is supposed to draw a line that is 6 inches long, how close the line actually measures to 6 inches

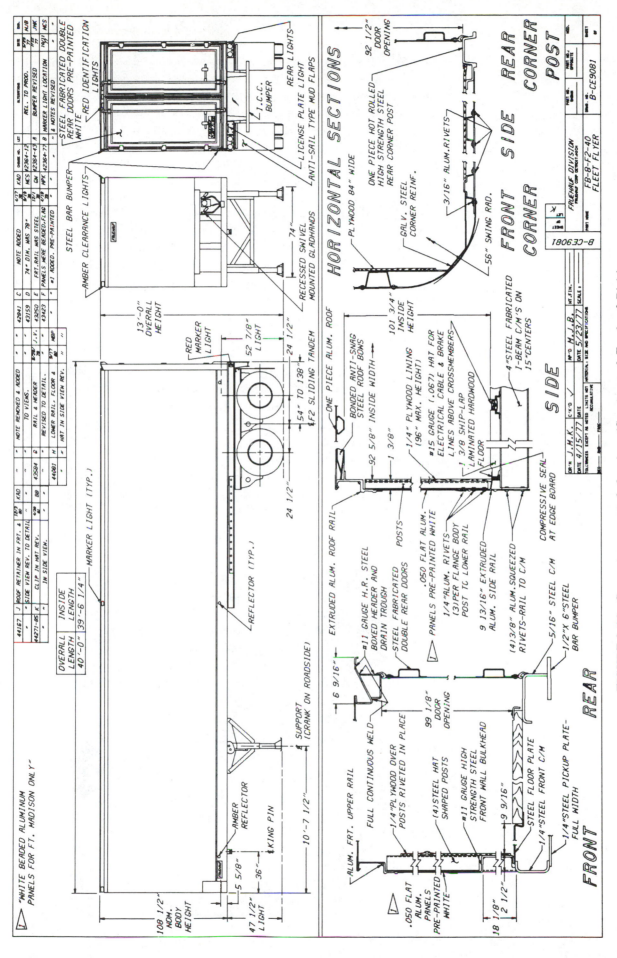

FIGURE 6-12 Computer-generated drawing. (Courtesy of Fruehauf Division of Fruehauf Corporation.)

determines how accurate the drafter has been. The same is true in computer-aided drafting. If the computer drafting technician commands the computer to draw a line that is 6 inches long, the line must measure 6 inches for the system to be considered accurate.

Repeatability concerns the computer's ability to retrace a line or series of lines exactly. It can only do this if it is able to return to precisely the same points which represent the end coordinates of the lines. If a plotter is able to do this, it is said to have a high degree of repeatability.

Repeatability is a problem for both manual and automated drafting. Manual drafters find it very difficult to retrace a line without adding length or width to it. It is also difficult to design a plotter that is able to do this. However, most computer-aided drafting systems are easily superior to manual drafting techniques in achieving repeatability.

Plotting Limitations and Paper Sizes

In manual drafting, the drafter is limited by the size of the drafting board surface and available sizes of paper. Most drafters have experienced trying to fit an E-size sheet of paper (34 × 44 inches) on a drafting board designed to accommodate D-size sheets (22 × 34 inches). This same problem exists in computer-aided drafting.

Plotters used in computer-aided drafting systems, just like drafting boards used in manual drafting rooms, come in a wide variety of sizes (Figures 6–13 through 6–15). Most flatbed plotters fall within the following range: 7 × 10 inches to 8 × 24 feet.

FIGURE 6-13 Flatbed plotter. (Courtesy of The Firestone Tire & Rubber Company.)

FIGURE 6-14 Flatbed plotter. (Courtesy of Applicon Incorporated.)

FIGURE 6-15 Flatbed plotter. (Courtesy of The Rust Engineering Company.)

Paper used on computer-aided drafting system plotters is the same as paper used for manual drafting. It is sized by both the American National Standards Institute (ANSI) and the International Standards Organization (ISO). ANSI designates paper sizes according to width and length in inches. ISO designates paper sizes according to width and length in millimetres. Figure 6-16 presents charts of the ANSI and ISO paper designations and the corresponding length and width dimensions.

Another limitation that affects both computer-aided drafting and manual drafting is the length of the precut sheets designated in the charts in Figure 6-16. Occasionally, a drafter will require a sheet

ISO	
Desig.	Size (mm)
A 4	210 x 297
A3	297 x 420
A2	420 x 594
A 1	594 x 841
A O	841 x 1189

ANSI	
Desig.	Size (in.)
A	$8\frac{1}{2}$ x 11
B	11 x 17
C	17 x 22
D	22 x 34
E	34 x 44

FIGURE 6-16   ANSI and ISO paper designations.

of paper that is longer than those available in precut form. In manual and automated drafting, this problem is solved in the same way. A roll of paper of the desired width may be selected and simply unrolled to the desired length in manual drafting or continuously fed across the plotter to achieve the desired length in computer-aided drafting. Most plotters in computer-aided drafting systems will accommodate both rolled paper and precut sheets.

MAKING DRAWINGS ON THE COMPUTER

At this point students have accumulated a sufficient background to begin a study of how common drafting tasks are performed on a computer-aided drafting system. This section describes the computer-aided drafting techniques used in performing such drafting tasks as lettering, linework, dimensioning, symbol creation, crosshatching, geometric constructions, scaling, drawing manipulation, and overlaying.

Lettering

The most common drafting task is lettering. Lettering is used for indicating dimensions, enumerating specifications, making notations, and entering on drawings all required alphanumeric characters. Most drawings involve a great deal of lettering. In manual drafting, lettering is a slow, arduous task and the quality of lettering has a tendency to decrease as the amount of lettering that has to be done on a drawing increases. This is because lettering must be hurried so as to not slow down production of the drawings and because the manual drafter simply gets tired. In computer-aided drafting, lettering is one of the fastest, easiest tasks the drafter has to perform.

Lettering is placed on drawings in computer-aided drafting by simply typing in the desired letters, words, notes, and so on (Figure 6–17). Computer-aided drafting lettering is fast, neat, easy to read, and available in a number of styles. Figures 6–18 and 6–19 present computer-generated drawings with large amounts of lettering. Notice how neat, clear, and legible the lettering is on each drawing.

Linework

Linework is another common drafting task. Beginning drafters learn to make object lines, hidden lines, leader lines, extension lines, centerlines, and dimension lines (Figure 6–20). All of the various types of lines can be made on a computer-aided drafting system. Lines may be created on a computer-aided drafting system in a number of ways. The most common way involves using a CRT workstation in conjunction with a digitizing tablet, electronic pen or cursor, and a menu (Figures 6–21 and 6–22).

The digitizing process enters lines as specified on a sketch or menu. Digitizing is very similar to tracing in manual drafting. Since

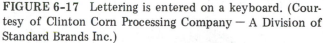

FIGURE 6-17 Lettering is entered on a keyboard. (Courtesy of Clinton Corn Processing Company — A Division of Standard Brands Inc.)

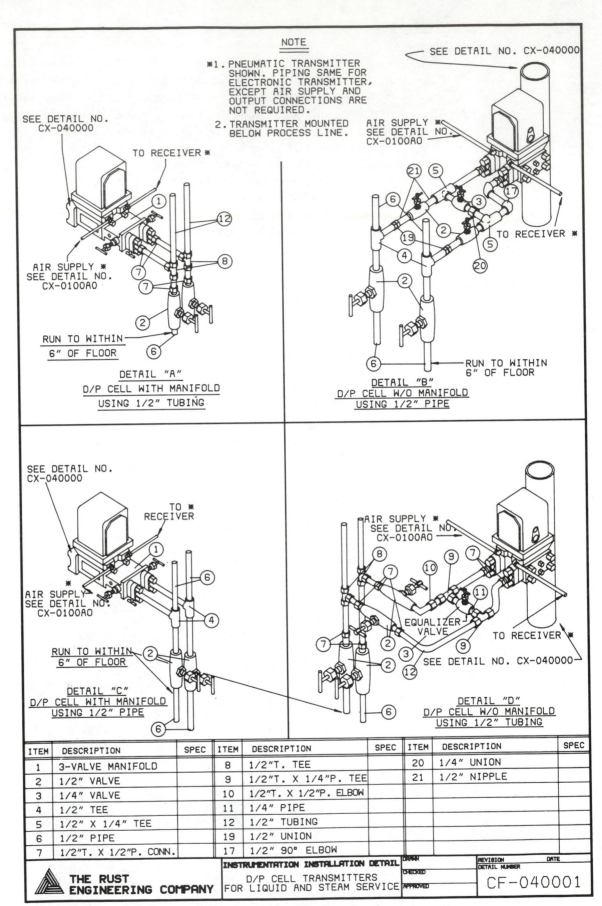

ITEM	DESCRIPTION	SPEC	ITEM	DESCRIPTION	SPEC	ITEM	DESCRIPTION	SPEC
1	3-VALVE MANIFOLD		8	1/2"T. TEE		20	1/4" UNION	
2	1/2" VALVE		9	1/2"T. X 1/4"P. TEE		21	1/2" NIPPLE	
3	1/4" VALVE		10	1/2"T. X 1/2"P. ELBOW				
4	1/2" TEE		11	1/4" PIPE				
5	1/2" X 1/4" TEE		12	1/2" TUBING				
6	1/2" PIPE		19	1/2" UNION				
7	1/2"T. X 1/2"P. CONN.		17	1/2" 90° ELBOW				

△ THE RUST ENGINEERING COMPANY

INSTRUMENTATION INSTALLATION DETAIL
D/P CELL TRANSMITTERS
FOR LIQUID AND STEAM SERVICE

DRAWN		REVISION	DATE
CHECKED		DETAIL NUMBER	
APPROVED		CF-040001	

FIGURE 6-18 Computer-generated drawings. (Courtesy of The Rust Engineering Company.)

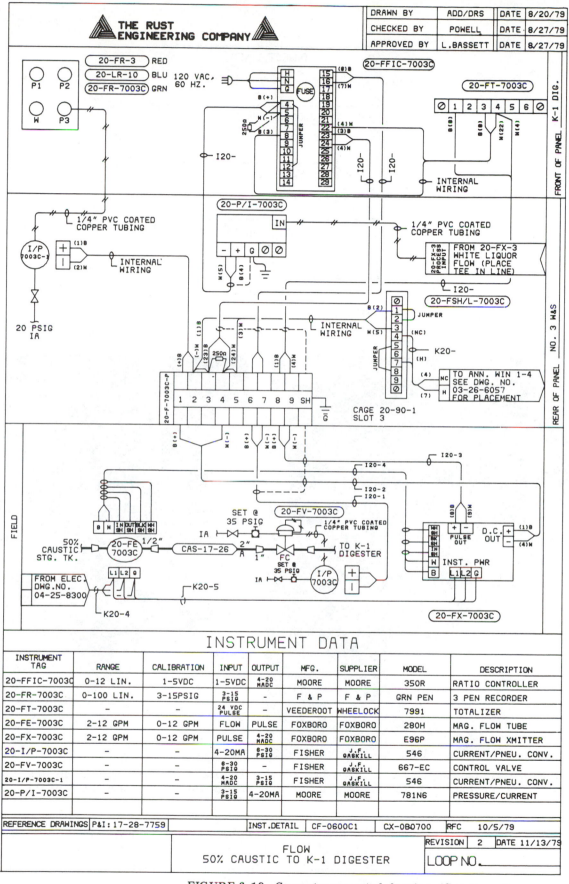

FIGURE 6-19 Computer-generated drawing. (Courtesy of The Rust Engineering Company.)

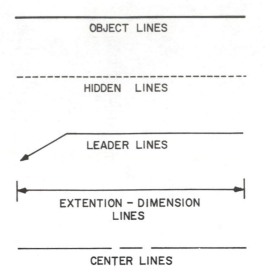

FIGURE 6-20   Line types used in drafting.

FIGURE 6-21   Entering lines into the system. (Courtesy of The Firestone Tire & Rubber Company.)

FIGURE 6-22   Entering lines into the system. (Courtesy of The Rust Engineering Company.)

the plotter in a computer-aided drafting system normally uses ink, the quality of lines on computer-generated drawings is generally better than that on manually prepared drawings. Notice the quality of the linework on the computer-generated drawings shown in Figure 6-23.

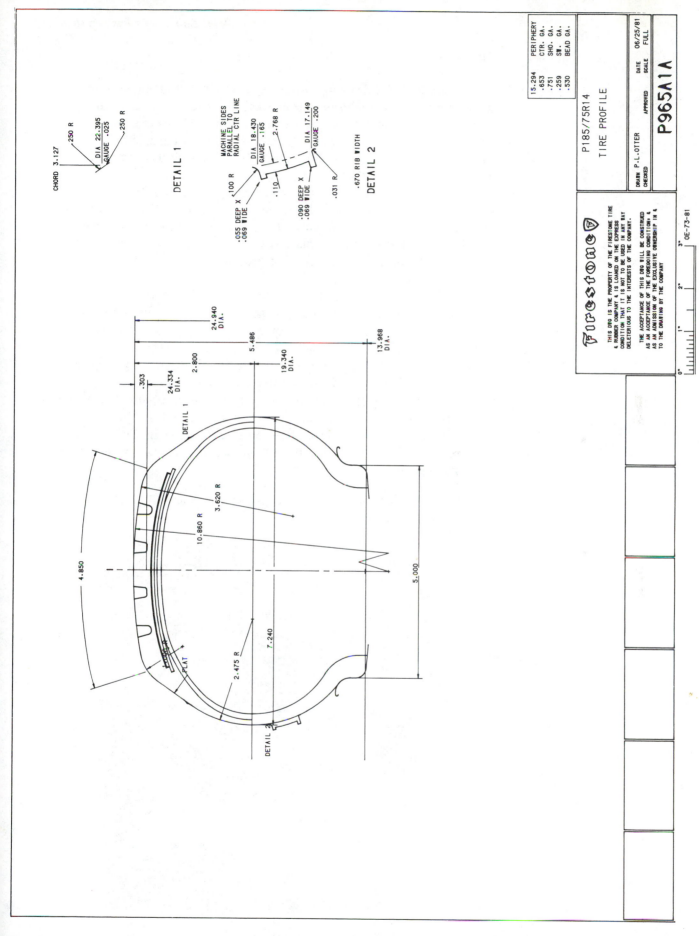

FIGURE 6-23 Computer-generated drawing. (Courtesy of The Firestone Tire & Rubber Company.)

Dimensioning

Dimensioning of a drawing in a computer-aided drafting system can be done either manually or automatically. Manual techniques involve the use of a menu to apply extension lines, dimension lines, and arrowheads in the appropriate places as the drawing is displayed on the CRT screen (Figure 6-24). The actual dimensions themselves are entered with the keyboard.

Software is available for certain computer-aided drafting applications that will automatically dimension drawings. The dimensions are calculated by the computer from the X-Y coordinates used in plotting and automatically placed in the appropriate places on the drawing. Automatic dimensioning can also include an automatic "follow-through" capability.

Follow-through is the process in which all the various changes that result from a dimensional change are made. Usually, one dimension on a drawing will affect other dimensions, so that one dimensional change may create several others. Learning to follow through and make all the changes that are generated by an initial change is a difficult task even for experienced drafters. The automatic follow-through capability of some computer-aided drafting systems ensures that all changes are made when a dimension is changed. Examine the dimensions on the drawing in Figure 6-25. If the 18.70-inch-diameter dimension were changed, what other dimensional changes should result?

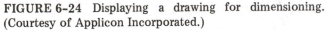

FIGURE 6-24 Displaying a drawing for dimensioning. (Courtesy of Applicon Incorporated.)

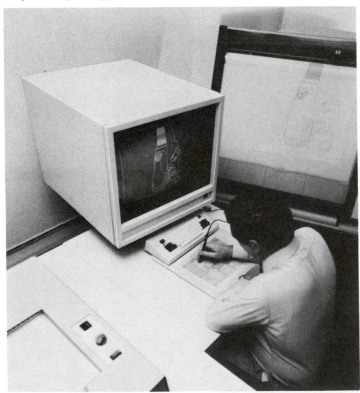

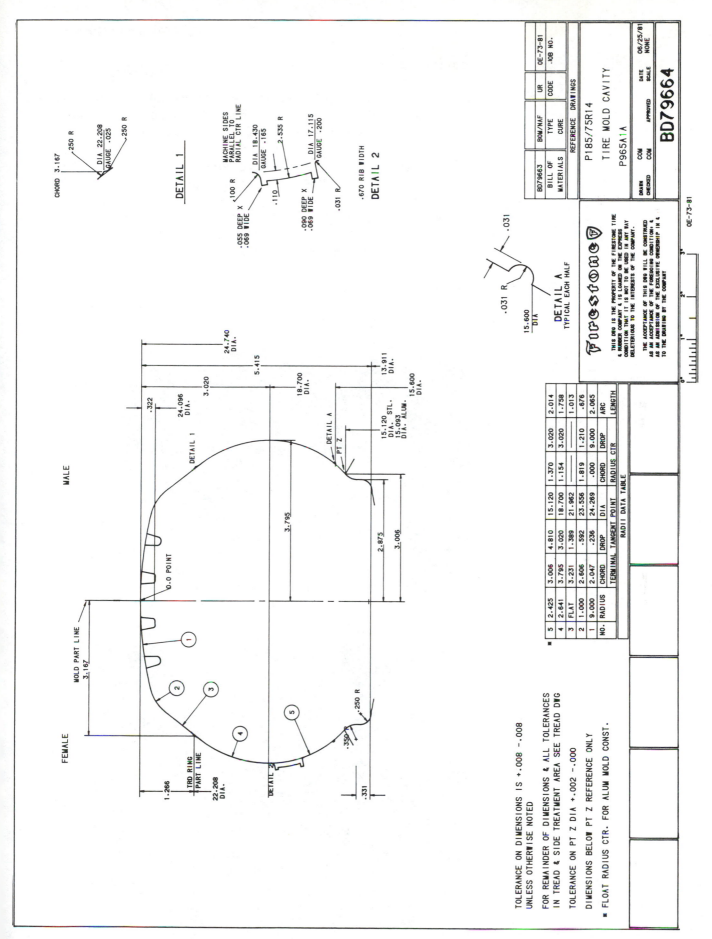

FIGURE 6-25 Computer-generated drawing. (Courtesy of The Firestone Tire & Rubber Company.)

153

Symbol Creation

Symbol creation is a common drafting task. In certain applications, such as piping drawings or electronics schematics, many symbols are used. In manual drafting the time involved in creating symbols that are used over and over again is decreased through the use of templates. There are circle templates, ellipse templates, electronics symbols templates, piping symbol templates, and numerous other types of templates for facilitating symbol creation in manual drafting.

Computer-aided drafting technicians use menus instead of templates. Actually, a menu is the computer-aided drafting equivalent of a template. A menu is a paper or plastic overlay of symbols which correspond to symbols that have been stored in the computer-aided drafting system's data base. Menus may be purchased as part of the computer-aided drafting system's software and/or developed locally by systems users.

FIGURE 6-26 Menus are used in conjunction with the digitizing process. (Courtesy of The Parsons Corporation.)

FIGURE 6-27 Menus can be used in conjunction with keyboards. (Courtesy of The Rust Engineering Company.)

There are two types of menus. One is used in conjunction with a digitizing tablet (Figure 6–26) and the other is used in conjunction with a keyboard (Figure 6–27). In either case, a menu allows a computer-aided drafting technician to enter symbols by simply activating the appropriate symbol on the menu with either an electronic pen or a cursor. Figure 6–28 contains a menu that comes with the AD 380 computer-aided drafting system manufactured by Auto-Trol Corporation.

FIGURE 6-28 Sample menu used on the Auto-Trol AD 380 computer-aided drafting system. (Courtesy of Auto-trol Technology Corporation.)

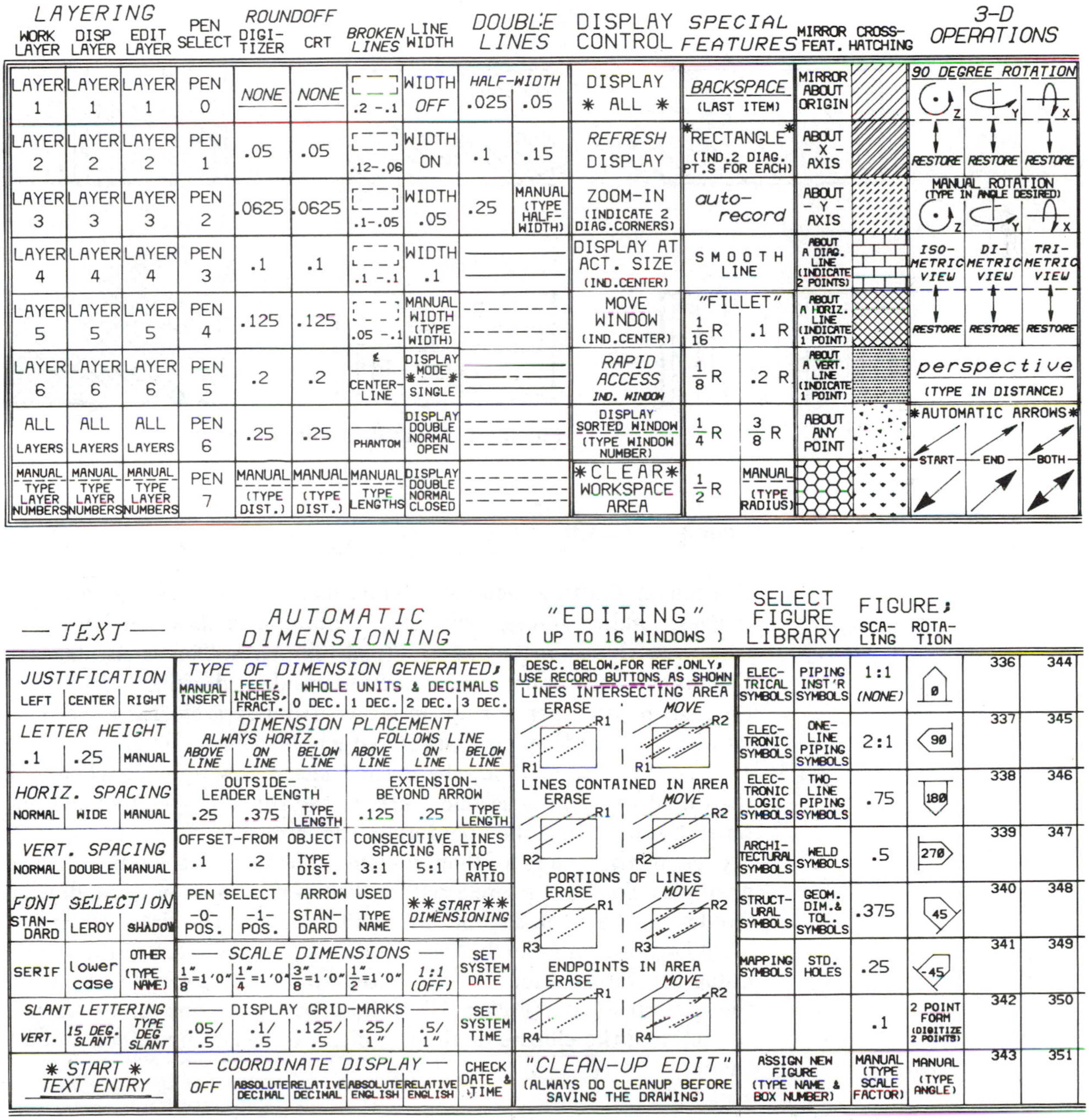

LAYERING — WORK LAYER	DISP LAYER	EDIT LAYER	PEN SELECT	ROUNDOFF DIGITIZER	ROUNDOFF CRT	BROKEN LINES	LINE WIDTH	DOUBLE LINES	DISPLAY CONTROL	SPECIAL FEATURES	MIRROR	CROSS-HATCHING	3-D OPERATIONS
LAYER 1	LAYER 1	LAYER 1	PEN 0	NONE	NONE	.2 –.1	WIDTH OFF	HALF-WIDTH .025 / .05	DISPLAY * ALL *	BACKSPACE (LAST ITEM)	MIRROR ABOUT ORIGIN		90 DEGREE ROTATION
LAYER 2	LAYER 2	LAYER 2	PEN 1	.05	.05	.12–.06	WIDTH ON	.1 / .15	REFRESH DISPLAY	"RECTANGLE" (IND. 2 DIAG. PT.S FOR EACH)	ABOUT –X– AXIS		RESTORE RESTORE RESTORE
LAYER 3	LAYER 3	LAYER 3	PEN 2	.0625	.0625	.1–.05	WIDTH .05	.25 / MANUAL (TYPE HALF-WIDTH)	ZOOM-IN (INDICATE 2 DIAG. CORNERS)	auto-record	ABOUT –Y– AXIS		MANUAL ROTATION (TYPE IN ANGLE DESIRED)
LAYER 4	LAYER 4	LAYER 4	PEN 3	.1	.1	.1 –.1	WIDTH .1		DISPLAY AT ACT. SIZE (IND. CENTER)	SMOOTH LINE	ABOUT A DIAG. LINE (INDICATE 2 POINTS)		ISO-METRIC VIEW / DI-METRIC VIEW / TRI-METRIC VIEW
LAYER 5	LAYER 5	LAYER 5	PEN 4	.125	.125	.05 –.1 MANUAL WIDTH (TYPE WIDTH)			MOVE WINDOW (IND. CENTER)	"FILLET" $\frac{1}{16}$R / .1 R	ABOUT A HORIZ. LINE (INDICATE 1 POINT)		RESTORE RESTORE RESTORE
LAYER 6	LAYER 6	LAYER 6	PEN 5	.2	.2	CENTER LINE	DISPLAY MODE * SINGLE *		RAPID ACCESS IND. WINDOW	$\frac{1}{8}$R / .2 R	ABOUT A VERT. LINE (INDICATE 1 POINT)		perspective (TYPE IN DISTANCE)
ALL LAYERS	ALL LAYERS	ALL LAYERS	PEN 6	.25	.25	PHANTOM	DISPLAY DOUBLE NORMAL OPEN		DISPLAY SORTED WINDOW (TYPE WINDOW NUMBER)	$\frac{1}{4}$R / $\frac{3}{8}$R	ABOUT ANY POINT		* AUTOMATIC ARROWS * START — END — BOTH
MANUAL TYPE LAYER NUMBERS	MANUAL TYPE LAYER NUMBERS	MANUAL TYPE LAYER NUMBERS	PEN 7	MANUAL (TYPE DIST.)	MANUAL (TYPE DIST.)	MANUAL TYPE LENGTHS	DISPLAY DOUBLE NORMAL CLOSED		* CLEAR * WORKSPACE AREA	$\frac{1}{2}$R / MANUAL (TYPE RADIUS)		MANUAL (TYPE RADIUS)	

— TEXT —	AUTOMATIC DIMENSIONING	"EDITING" (UP TO 16 WINDOWS)	SELECT FIGURE LIBRARY	FIGURE SCALING	ROTATION	FIG.
JUSTIFICATION: LEFT / CENTER / RIGHT	TYPE OF DIMENSION GENERATED: MANUAL INSERT / FEET, INCHES, FRACT. / WHOLE UNITS & DECIMALS: 0 DEC. / 1 DEC. / 2 DEC. / 3 DEC.	DESC. BELOW FOR REF. ONLY, USE RECORD BUTTONS AS SHOWN — LINES INTERSECTING AREA: ERASE (R1) / MOVE (R2)	ELECTRICAL SYMBOLS / PIPING INST'R SYMBOLS	1:1 (NONE)	0	336 / 344
LETTER HEIGHT: .1 / .25 / MANUAL	DIMENSION PLACEMENT: ALWAYS HORIZ. (ABOVE LINE / ON LINE / BELOW LINE) — FOLLOWS LINE (ABOVE LINE / ON LINE / BELOW LINE)	LINES CONTAINED IN AREA: ERASE / MOVE (R2)	ELECTRONIC SYMBOLS / ONE-LINE PIPING SYMBOLS	2:1	90	337 / 345
HORIZ. SPACING: NORMAL / WIDE / MANUAL	OUTSIDE-LEADER LENGTH: .25 / .375 / TYPE LENGTH — EXTENSION-BEYOND ARROW: .125 / .25 / TYPE LENGTH	PORTIONS OF LINES: ERASE (R1) / MOVE (R2) — R3 / R3	ELECTRONIC LOGIC SYMBOLS / TWO-LINE PIPING SYMBOLS	.75	180	338 / 346
VERT. SPACING: NORMAL / DOUBLE / MANUAL	OFFSET-FROM OBJECT: .1 / .2 / TYPE DIST. — CONSECUTIVE LINES SPACING RATIO: 3:1 / 5:1 / TYPE RATIO	R2 / R2	ARCHITECTURAL SYMBOLS / WELD SYMBOLS	.5	270	339 / 347
FONT SELECTION: STANDARD / LEROY / SHADOW	PEN SELECT: –0– POS. / –1– POS. — ARROW USED: STANDARD / TYPE NAME — ** START ** DIMENSIONING	ENDPOINTS IN AREA: ERASE (R1) / MOVE (R2) — R3 / R3	STRUCTURAL SYMBOLS / GEOM. DIM.& TOL. SYMBOLS	.375	45	340 / 348
SERIF / lower case / OTHER (TYPE NAME)	SCALE DIMENSIONS: $\frac{1}{8}"=1'0"$ / $\frac{1}{4}"=1'0"$ / $\frac{3}{8}"=1'0"$ / $\frac{1}{2}"=1'0"$ / 1:1 (OFF) — SET SYSTEM DATE	R4 / R4	MAPPING SYMBOLS / STD. HOLES	.25	-45	341 / 349
SLANT LETTERING: VERT. / 15 DEG. SLANT / TYPE DEG SLANT	DISPLAY GRID-MARKS: .05/.5 / .1/1 / .125/1.25 / .25/2.5 / .5/1" — SET SYSTEM TIME			.1	2 POINT FORM (DIGITIZE 2 POINTS)	342 / 350
* START * TEXT ENTRY	COORDINATE DISPLAY: OFF / ABSOLUTE DECIMAL / RELATIVE DECIMAL / ABSOLUTE ENGLISH / RELATIVE ENGLISH — CHECK DATE & TIME	"CLEAN-UP EDIT" (ALWAYS DO CLEANUP BEFORE SAVING THE DRAWING)	ASSIGN NEW FIGURE (TYPE NAME & BOX NUMBER)	MANUAL (TYPE SCALE FACTOR)	MANUAL (TYPE ANGLE)	343 / 351

Crosshatching

Crosshatching is used in drafting to indicate section cuts and to make the symbols that distinguish between certain materials (Figure 6-29). In manual drafting, crosshatching is a slow, arduous process. Uniformity of spacing between crosshatching lines is very difficult to achieve. In computer-aided drafting, crosshatching is much simpler.

Crosshatching is accomplished in computer-aided drafting by simply outlining (defining) the area to be crosshatched and inputting the crosshatching command. The various types of crosshatching may be made part of a menu so that the computer-aided drafting technician need only touch a block on a menu to crosshatch the desired portion of the drawing.

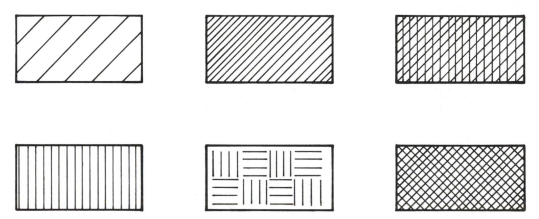

FIGURE 6-29   Crosshatching symbols.

Geometric Constructions

In manual drafting, geometric constructions such as squares, rectangles, circles, ellipses, and other common shapes can be drawn from scratch or created using special templates. This is also true of computer-aided drafting. In computer-aided drafting, frequently used geometric shapes may be drawn from scratch using the digitizing process or they may be entered whole using a menu.

In the first method, the desired shape is simply sketched and then digitized. In the second method, the shape is specified and entered by activating the appropriate shape on the menu. The size of the geometric shape is then specified through the keyboard. For example: To draw a circle with a diameter of 6 inches, the drafter would use the menu to input the center point of the circle. He or she would then use the keyboard to indicate the diameter of the circle. Using this information, the computer would then generate a circle of the prescribed size (Figure 6-30). Similarly, polygons can be created by defining the ellipses or circles which can be circumscribed around them.

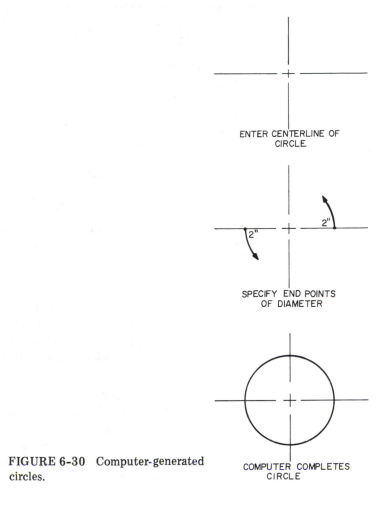

ENTER CENTERLINE OF
CIRCLE

SPECIFY END POINTS
OF DIAMETER

COMPUTER COMPLETES
CIRCLE

FIGURE 6-30 Computer-generated circles.

Drawing Manipulation

Drawing manipulation functions in computer-aided drafting include zoom-in, zoom-out, mirror, rotate, and scale. Manipulation of drawings takes place while the drawing is displayed on the CRT screen. Each time the drawing is changed in any way, an original drawing reflecting the new change can be obtained by simply activating the plot command on the CRT keyboard.

Zoom-in allows a drafter to zero in on a certain portion of a drawing for a close-up view (Figure 6–31). The zoom-in function is accomplished by simply pressing the zoom-in key on the CRT keyboard. Each time the zoom-in button is pressed, the picture will be displayed successively larger and closer. Some computer-aided drafting systems have a capability of 15 successive zoom-ins. This is a particularly valuable function because while the computer has zoomed in on a particular portion of a drawing, the plotter can be commanded to draw that piece. This results in a blown-up detail of just the desired piece of the drawing. This is important because the need for blown-up details of isolated portions of very complicated drawings is very common in drafting.

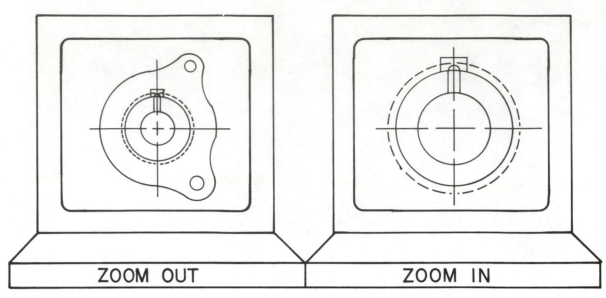

ZOOM OUT   ZOOM IN

FIGURE 6-31   Zoom-in function.

Zoom-out is just the opposite of zoom-in and is handled in the same way on the keyboard. This function allows the drafter to return to normal after having zoomed in and to zoom out even farther to achieve a wider-angle perspective on a drawing.

Mirroring is another valuable computer-aided drafting manipulation capability that cuts down on drafting time. Many objects drawn by drafters are symmetrical about an X or Y axis. When this is the case, one half of the object may be created on the CRT screen through digitizing or other input techniques. The second half of the drawing is then obtained by simply pressing the mirror button (Figure 6-32).

FIGURE 6-32   Mirror function.

STEP ONE   STEP TWO

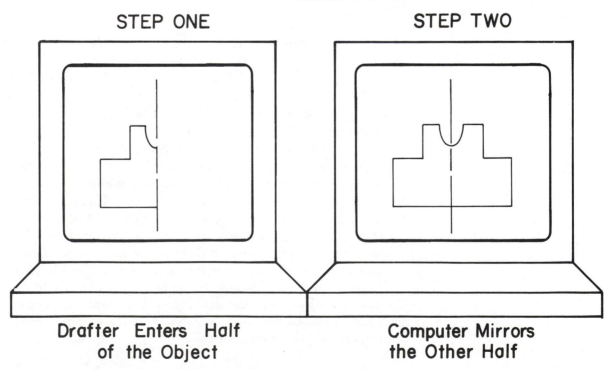

Drafter Enters Half   Computer Mirrors
of the Object   the Other Half

The most important manipulation function for drafters involved in three-dimensional drawings is the *rotate* function. In drafting it is very common to need several different three-dimensional views of an object to show how it would appear when viewed from different angles (Figure 6–33). In manual drafting this means that the drafter must start each successive drawing over from scratch to obtain the desired angle of display. This is a particularly time-consuming chore. In computer-aided drafting, revolving drawings to achieve different angles is much easier.

In computer-aided drafting, the drafter simply enters the object to be drawn at various angles and displays it on the CRT screen. He or she may then press the rotate button on the CRT keyboard to rotate the object to different angles. Each time the object is rotated to a desired angle, the plotter may be activated to obtain an original drawing of the object at the desired angle. In this way, many drawings of the object from many different angles may be completed in the time it would take to create even one drawing manually.

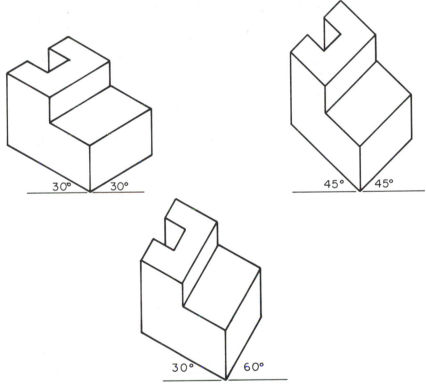

FIGURE 6-33 Rotate function.

Scaling is another useful computer-aided drafting function. It allows the drafter to increase or decrease the size of the object as it is displayed on the CRT screen (Figure 6–34). This is accomplished by entering a scale factor (2×, 4×, 0.5×, etc.) and then entering the object itself in actual size. As the drawing is input, the computer will automatically scale it to the desired size. This type of scaling has to do with changing the scale of a drawing which is displayed on the CRT screen from full size to some other size, either larger or smaller. Scaling such as that which the manual drafter is used to doing with

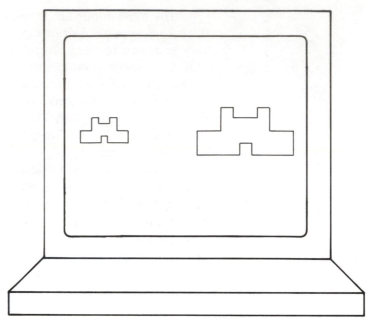

FIGURE 6–34   Scaling function.

an architect's, engineer's, or metric scale may also be handled very simply on a computer-aided drafting system.

Scaling

Scaling in drafting is the process by which very large objects such as buildings, ships, machines, automobiles, and aircraft are drawn on relatively small sheets of paper. For example: In drawing the floor plan for a house, the house might be 30 feet wide and 60 feet long or even larger. The paper on which the floor plan is to be drawn might be only 17 inches wide and 22 inches long. Obviously, the floor plan will have to be scaled down in order to fit on the available size of paper.

The manual drafter would take an architect's scale, select an appropriate scale (usually $\frac{1}{4}$ inch = 1 foot for floor plans), and draw the floor plan. Because the builders would act on the dimensions given rather than the actual size of the drawing, the house would be properly built. In computer-aided drafting, the problem of selecting a scale that will make the object fit on the available size of paper is eliminated. In fact, scaling on most computer-aided drafting systems is automatic.

Rather than selecting a particular scale in computer-aided drafting, the drafter simply inputs the size of the drafting surface to be used on the available paper. The computer automatically scales all graphic data so that they fit within the prescribed drafting area. The drafter then is always thinking in and using full-size dimensions, and the computer is making the necessary adjustments. This is much less confusing than manual scaling.

The computer on most modern computer-aided drafting systems will scale automatically. However, for depth of understanding, the drafter should know what the computer is doing when it scales a drawing. When the computer scales input down to fit within a prescribed drafting area, it is actually converting computer units to user units. Computer units are units of varying length that divide the system's plotting surfaces (CRT screen or plotter surface) into increments along the X and Y axes. User units are such things as feet, inches, and millimetres. The plotting surface of a computer-aided drafting system may be divided into, say, 100 units on the Y axis and 200 on the X axis. Regardless of the actual size of the plotting surface, it will have 100 units in the Y and 200 units in the X if that is how the surface has been divided. The number of units in each axis varies from system to system (Figure 6–35).

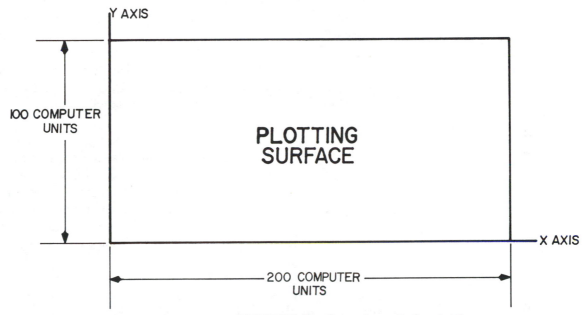

FIGURE 6-35   Computer units for plotting.

An inch is always an inch and a millimetre is always a millimetre, but computer units are relative to the size of the plotting area and so vary in actual length. For example: If two plotting surfaces are divided into 100 Y units and 150 X units but one surface is larger than the other, the units of the larger surface will be longer than those of the smaller. This principle is illustrated in Figure 6–36 with two different plotting areas, each having 100 units in the Y axis and 200 units in the X axis. The units for plotting area A are obviously shorter than those for area B. However, both plotting areas are divided into the same number of units.

When a drafter inputs user units such as feet, inches, or millimetres, the computer actually performs the necessary calculations for converting computer units into user units and scales the input down to fit into the prescribed drafting area. On earlier units, drafters had to perform these computations themselves. However, modern computer-aided drafting systems perform this cumbersome task automatically.

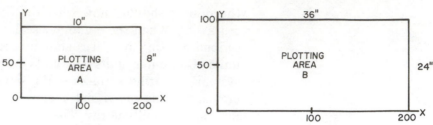

FIGURE 6-36   Computer units can vary in length.

Overlaying

Prior to the advent of computer-aided drafting, an effective work- and timesaving technique for manual drafting was overlaying. Overlaying eliminates the need for repetition of drawing by laying successive sheets on top of a standard base sheet and drawing only those parts of the drawing that apply to a given overlay. For example: If a manual drafter were preparing a set of house plans, he or she would draw a floor plan, an electrical plan, a plumbing plan, and a ductwork plan. In each case, the starting point for each plan would be the floor plan minus the dimensions.

In order to draw the electrical, plumbing, and ductwork plans, the drafter must recreate the floor plan each time. It may either be redrawn each time, which is very time consuming, or created by running sepias of the floor plan and using them for the base of the electrical, plumbing, and duct plans. The latter method is faster than redrawing the floor plan each time. However, sepias do not afford drafters the quality of linework and printing that the original drafting vellum or polyester film will.

In manual drafting, this problem is eliminated by overlaying. Overlaying means using the floor plan as a base and laying a clean sheet on top of it for the electrical, plumbing, or duct plan. In each case, only the electrical, plumbing, or ducting information is drawn on the overlays. The floor plan is not redrawn. A print of the electrical, plumbing, or duct plan is obtained by overlaying the appropriate plan on the floor plan during the printing process. This technique is particularly valuable in printed-circuit-board drafting.

Computer-aided drafting systems also have an overlaying capability. Some systems can handle up to 15 different layers at one time. Some can even plot several layers at once, each in a different color of ink. Each individual layer is simply input into the computer in the same way that single-layer drawings are entered. Once they have been input, layers may be displayed one at a time or in any combination desired. The principle of overlaying is illustrated in Figure 6-37.

OTHER COMPUTER-AIDED DRAFTING PROCESSES

When the term "drafting" is mentioned, one usually thinks only of those tasks which are performed in creating finished working drawings. These are the tasks that have been dealt with in the preceding sections of this chapter. However, there is more to the drafting process than the creation of original drawings. Other important

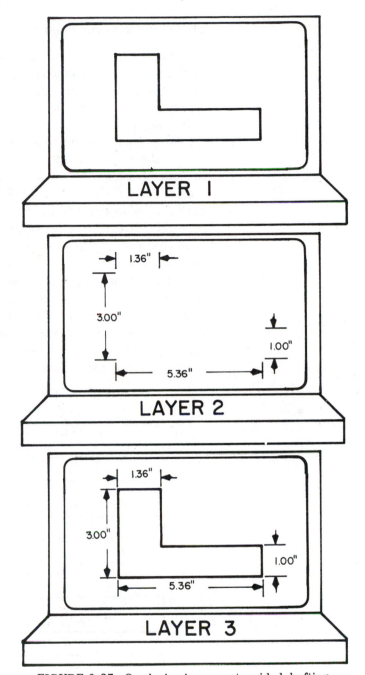

FIGURE 6-37 Overlaying in computer-aided drafting.

processes that fall under the umbrella of drafting are: checking of drawings, correcting of drawings, and storing of drawings.

These processes must be performed whether the techniques used in creating drawings are manual techniques or automated techniques. In order to fully understand how these processes are performed on a computer-aided drafting system, it is necessary to compare these processes in an automated setting with the same processes in a manual setting. In this section you will learn how to accomplish the checking, correcting, and storage of drawings in a computer-aided drafting setting as well as how these things are done in a manual drafting setting.

Checking and Correcting Drawings

Checking of drawings is an important step in the overall development of drawings in both manual and computer-aided drafting. Just as the "boss" will always proofread a letter that his or her secretary has typed before signing it, the designer must always check drawings before signing them.

Checking is done to ensure that the drafter has correctly converted the raw data into finished drawings. A number of different aspects of a drawing must be checked. Is the drawing properly arranged on the sheet? Are all dimensions correct? Does the drawing convey the intent of the designer? Are all notes on the drawing correct? Have all pertinent drafting standards been observed? All these questions must be answered about every drawing that is produced either manually or on a computer-aided drafting system.

The checker will go over a drawing and examine it closely. All mistakes will be noted and the drawing will be returned to the drafter for corrections. Figure 6-38 compares the steps in the checking-correcting process for manual and computer-aided drafting. A drawing such as the one shown in Figure 6-39 has usually been through several corrections before it is finally completed.

FIGURE 6-38   Checking-correcting process.

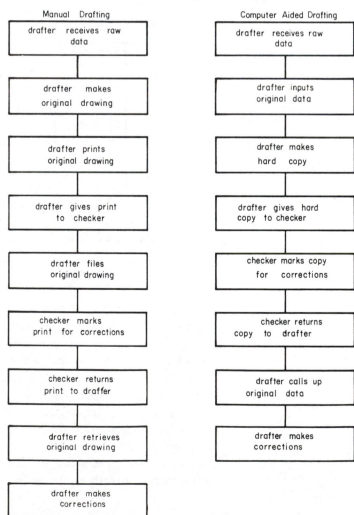

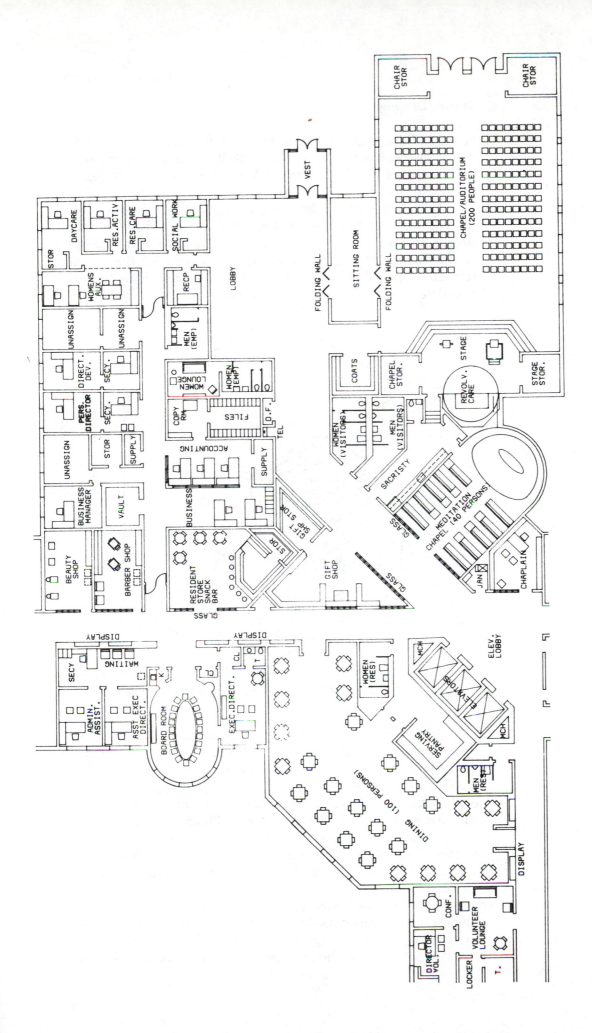

PARTIAL FLOOR PLAN

SCALE 1/8"=1'-0"

FIGURE 6-39 Computer-generated drawing. (Courtesy of Auto-trol Technology Corporation.)

Storing Drawings

Storage of drawings is a problem in every drafting department. Companies involved in manual drafting usually store their original drawings in special metal filing drawers which allow the drawings to lie flat (Figure 6-40).

These filing drawers are good for manual storage and will even protect drawings from fire within certain limits. However, manual storage has two major drawbacks: (1) constant retrieving and refiling of drawings leads to eventual deterioration and even the occasional ruin of original drawings; and (2) over the years, filing drawers accumulate, requiring more and more space.

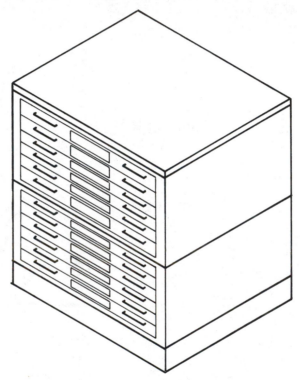

FIGURE 6-40 Filing drawers for storing drawing manually.

Drawing storage is one of a computer-aided drafting system's strongest selling points. Since drawings are stored on tape or disks rather than as originals, the two drawbacks listed above for manual drafting are eliminated for computer-aided drafting. Filing a drawing in computer-aided drafting is as simple as pressing a button, and whatever appears on the screen is stored (Figure 6-41).

Retrieving drawings from the file (storage) is again simply a matter of inputting the proper command. When this is done, the desired drawing will be displayed on the CRT screen in a matter of seconds (Figure 6-42).

Computer-aided drafting storage techniques also have the advantage of requiring considerably less space than manual techniques. In addition, duplicate tape files can be easily made and stored in a fireproof safe as protection against fire, theft, or natural disaster.

FIGURE 6-41 Storing drawings by pressing a button. (Courtesy of Auto-trol Technology Corporation.)

FIGURE 6-42 Recalling and displaying stored drawings. (Courtesy of Auto-trol Technology Corporation.)

SUMMARY AND REVIEW

- Computer-aided drafting involves three basic operations: input, manipulation, and output of data.

- For inputting and manipulating data, drafters use CRT keyboards, digitizing tablets, electronic pens, cursors, and menus.

- For outputting data, drafters use printers, hard-copy units, and plotters.

- Computer-aided drafting systems convert electrical impulses into graphical data by plotting X-Y coordinates on a Cartesian coordinate system.

- In computer-aided drafting, the computer actually creates lines by plotting the coordinates of the end points of the lines and filling in between them.

- All geometric shapes used in drafting are actually formed by a series of short lines. This includes such shapes as arcs, curves, and circles.

- Resolution is the degree of smoothness the computer-aided drafting system's plotter is able to achieve in plotting arcs, curves, and circles.

- The more points per inch that the computer plots, the higher the resolution of the drawings plotted.

- The accuracy of a computer-aided drafting system's plotter is a measure of how close it comes to creating lines which are actually the length they are supposed to be.

- Repeatability is a computer-aided drafting system's ability to retrace lines that have been drawn without adding length or width to them.

- Flatbed plotters for computer-aided drafting systems range in size from 7×10 inches to 8×24 feet.

- ANSI paper sizes are (in inches): A, $8\frac{1}{2} \times 11$; B, 11×17; C, 17×22; D, 22×34; and E, 34×44.

- ISO paper sizes are (in millimetres): A4, 210×297; A3, 297×420; A2, 420×594; A1, 594×841; and A0, 841×1189.
- Lettering is accomplished in a computer-aided drafting system by typing in the desired characters.

- In computer-aided drafting, the most common method for producing the lines that make up drawings is digitizing. This process is very similar to tracing in manual drafting.

- Dimensions in computer-aided drafting may be done automatically or they may be entered through the CRT keyboard.

- In automatic dimensioning the computer calculates dimensions using the X-Y coordinates that were used to plot the lines on the drawing.

- Menus are used in computer-aided drafting for symbol creation in much the same way that templates are used in manual drafting.

- Crosshatching is accomplished in computer-aided drafting by defining the area to be crosshatched and then inputting the appropriate crosshatching symbol.

- Drawing manipulation capabilities on most computer-aided

drafting systems include zoom-in, zoom-out, mirror, rotate, and scale.

- A drafter causes a computer-aided drafting system's plotter to scale input automatically by defining the area of the drafting surface.

- In scaling graphical input, the computer is actually converting computer units to user units, such as feet, inches, or millimetres.

- Computer-aided drafting systems are capable of handling several layers of drawings at one time and displaying them simultaneously in any desired combination.

- In computer-aided drafting the checking–correcting process proceeds as follows: (1) the drafter creates an original drawing; (2) the drafter makes a hard copy of a drawing; (3) the drafter gives the hard copy to the checker; (4) the checker marks the hard copy for corrections; (5) the checker returns the marked-up copy to the drafter for corrections; (6) the drafter calls up the original data on the CRT screen; (7) the drafter makes all required corrections.

- In computer-aided drafting, drawings are stored on tape or disks, which requires much less room and involves much less wear and tear than filing original drawings in filing drawers as is done in manual drafting.

SELF-TEST Directions

Respond to the following questions without referring to the chapter. When you have answered all questions, check your answers by referring to the appropriate sections of the chapter. Reread any section covering questions that were missed several times before proceeding to the next chapter.

1. Indicate whether each of the following statements is true or false.
   a. All geometric shapes used in drafting are actually formed by straight lines, except arcs, curves, and circles.
   b. The more points per inch the computer plots in creating a circle, the higher the resolution of the circle.
   c. The only way to enter dimensions on a computer-aided drafting system is through the keyboard.

2. Explain how a plotter in a computer-aided drafting system converts electrical impulses into graphical data.

3. Explain how the plotter for a computer-aided drafting system actually plots a line.

4. Explain the term "accuracy" as it pertains to computer-aided drafting.

5. Explain the term "repeatability" as it applies to computer-aided drafting.

6. Explain how lettering is done on a computer-aided drafting system.

7. Explain the digitizing process as used in computer-aided drafting.

8. Explain how the computer is able to perform automatic dimensioning on a drawing.

9. Explain how a drafter would crosshatch a portion of a drawing on a computer-aided drafting system.

10. Explain how a drafter causes the computer to scale graphical input properly when making drawings on a computer-aided drafting system.

11. Explain what the computer actually does when it scales graphical input.

12. Explain how drawings are stored in a computer-aided drafting system. What are the advantages of the storage methods used in computer-aided drafting?

13. Computer-aided drafting involves three basic operations. What are they?

14. List five things computer-aided drafting technicians use for inputting data into a system.

15. List three things computer-aided drafting technicians use for outputting data.

16. What is the size range for flatbed plotters used in computer-aided drafting systems?

17. Name five drawing manipulation functions common to most computer-aided drafting systems.

18. Match the following ANSI paper designations with their corresponding sizes in inches:

Paper designation	Size (inches)
A	11 × 17
B	34 × 44
C	$8\frac{1}{2}$ × 11
D	17 × 22
E	22 × 34

19. Match the following ISO paper designations with their corresponding sizes in millimetres:

Paper designation	Size (millimetres)
A4	594 × 841
A3	210 × 297
A2	297 × 420
A1	841 × 1189
A0	420 × 594

20. Make a flowchart that will illustrate all the steps, in order, that take place in the checking–correcting process in computer-aided drafting.

21. Define the term "resolution."

22. Define the term "menu."

7

EMPLOYMENT AS A COMPUTER–AIDED DRAFTING TECHNICIAN

OBJECTIVES   Upon completion of this chapter, you will be able to:
1. Explain how to prepare for the job search.
2. Explain how to identify potential employers of computer drafting technicians.
3. Explain how to contact potential employers about a job.
4. Explain how to keep a job and advance in it.

PREPARING FOR THE JOB SEARCH   The drafter who has acquired job-entry-level skills in a particular drafting field and has added the knowledge of computer-aided drafting presented in this book is ready to begin a career as a computer drafting technician. However, knowing how to do a job is not enough. One must also know how to find a job, get a job, and keep a job. The purpose of this chapter is to help drafting students develop the job-seeking skills necessary to be able to begin their careers as computer drafting technicians immediately after completing school. Before beginning the job search, drafting students should attend to some important preliminaries that will make the job search a less frustrating, more productive process.

The Job Seeker's Commandments

The first step in preparing for the job search is to broaden one's employment potential to the maximum by learning the "job seeker's commandments" (Figure 7–1). The first rule concerns relocating for employment. Accepting this principle is critical to the success of a job search. One of the most important factors in determining how successful a person will be in a given occupation is that person's mobility.

Often, the community immediately surrounding an educational institution will become glutted with skilled workers. This is because every year another class of students from the community graduates and hopes to find employment there. Eventually, the number of job seekers has to exceed the number of jobs. This is especially true of small rural communities with little or no industrial base. When this happens, the logical alternative is for the job seeker to relocate to a community where jobs are available.

The second rule involves learning to market one's skills. Drafting skills in a particular drafting field, especially those that have been broadened to include computer drafting skills, are badly needed in the world of work. However, if a job seeker does not learn how to market these skills, he or she may not be able to get a job and practice them. Learning to market one's skills means learning to identify potential employers, write an impressive résumé, write eye-catching letters of inquiry, successfully conduct job interviews, properly complete job applications, and several other important skills.

The third rule admonishes drafters to be willing to start at the bottom and work up. This is important because many drafters, regardless of how well they have been trained, will be expected to start at entry-level positions and gradually work their way up as experience is gained.

The fourth rule encourages job seekers to be positive and assertive during the job search. This is critical because it takes a positive attitude to bring positive results. Most job openings will attract more

FIGURE 7–1   Job seeker's commandments.

THE JOB SEEKER'S COMMANDMENTS

1. Be willing to relocate for employment. If you want a good job, you must be willing to go where the good jobs are in your field.

2. Learn to market your skills. Knowing how to find, get, and keep a job is almost as important as knowing how to do a job.

3. Be willing to start at the bottom in your occupation and work your way up.

4. Be positive and assertive during the job search. It will take a positive attitude and an assertive approach to break the "experience barrier."

5. Above all, do not become frustrated! It may take many interviews before you finally get the job you want.

than one applicant. If a job seeker were to appear timid or unsure during an interview, his or her chances of getting the job would not be enhanced.

The final rule is probably the most important for the inexperienced computer-aided drafting technician. Trying to break into the job market without experience can be a frustrating task. It might take the inexperienced job seeker many interviews before he or she is offered a job. This should be expected. Every interview, regardless of how many it takes, should be approached with a positive manner as if it is the one in which a job offer will be made.

Once a student has learned the job seeker's commandments, he or she is ready to take the next step in preparing for the job search. This involves preparing for the possibility of having to relocate for employment. If handled properly, relocating for employment can be a relatively simple task.

The Relocation Checklist

The first rule in the job seeker's commandments encourages job seekers to go where the best jobs are in their career field. This is sound advice. However, before accepting an out-of-town position, the drafter should examine the host city carefully. The cost of living, wages, climate, taxes, recreation, public utilities, transportation, and educational opportunities should all be examined for any city considered as a relocation possibility.

The relocation checklist in Figure 7–2 will assist job seekers in conducting a thorough, systematic investigation of any city prior to accepting a job there. The checklist is divided into four parts: taxes, housing, transportation, and general considerations. Answers to questions listed in each category may be found in the *World Almanac*, which is available in most libraries. The chamber of commerce for the city in question will also provide information needed to complete a relocation checklist.

IDENTIFYING POTENTIAL EMPLOYERS

A well-prepared job seeker is ready to go wherever the best jobs are in his or her field. In drafting, where the best jobs are means the larger cities in each state and the areas with a solid industrial base. After selecting the city in which to seek employment, the next step is to identify potential employers within that city. Potential employers of computer drafting technicians are the same as potential employers of conventional drafters, with the possible exception that at the present state of technological development, larger companies are leading the way in converting to computer-aided drafting.

If a computer drafting technician wished to be an architectural drafter, he or she would seek employment with architectural firms. The firms most likely to have a computer drafting system will be the larger firms. Computer drafting technicians wishing to be mechanical drafters will seek employment with the larger manufacturing firms, civil drafters with the larger civil engineering firms, and so on.

```
┌─────────────────────────────────────────────────────────────────┐
│                                                                   │
│                      RELOCATION CHECKLIST                         │
│                                                                   │
│   Taxes                                                           │
│                                                                   │
│   1.  Is there a state income tax? If so, how much is it?         │
│   2.  Is there a city or municipal income tax? If so, how much is it? │
│   3.  How much is the state sales tax?                            │
│   4.  What are the property tax rates?                            │
│   5.  How much homestead exemption is allowed on property taxes?  │
│                                                                   │
│   Housing                                                         │
│                                                                   │
│   1.  What is the availability and cost of housing for buyers?    │
│   2.  What is the availability and cost of rental units?          │
│   3.  How much does it cost to initiate such services as electricity, water, sewage, │
│       telephone, garbage collection, and television?             │
│   4.  How much will it cost to move your furniture, clothing, and household │
│       belongings?                                                 │
│                                                                   │
│   Transportation                                                  │
│                                                                   │
│   1.  Is public transportation available? At what cost?           │
│   2.  What is the current price of gasoline?                      │
│   3.  What is the cost of normal automobile maintenance?          │
│   4.  How much driving will be required to and from work?         │
│                                                                   │
│   General Considerations                                          │
│                                                                   │
│   1.  What is the relative cost of a typical grocery basket of food? │
│   2.  What is the relative cost of clothing?                      │
│   3.  What types of recreational activities are available?        │
│   4.  What type of educational opportunities are available for continuing │
│       education?                                                  │
│   5.  What is the typical weather during each season?             │
│   6.  What is the quality of the public school system for children? │
│                                                                   │
└─────────────────────────────────────────────────────────────────┘
```

FIGURE 7-2 Relocation checklist.

Most people are familiar with want ads, public employment offices, private employment offices, and the various other traditional sources of help in locating potential employers. However, most people are not familiar with what are probably the two most effective sources of assistance available to job-seeking computer drafting technicians: chamber of commerce industrial directories and telephone directories.

Chamber of Commerce Industrial Directories

One of the most effective sources of assistance for identifying potential employers in a given city is the chamber of commerce industrial directory for that city. Almost every city in the country has a chamber of commerce, and almost every chamber publishes and distributes its own industrial directory. Directories range in size from small typewritten tabloids to large commercially produced books. Some cities provide their directories free upon request, whereas others charge for them. In either case, a directory may be obtained by writing or calling the chamber of commerce for the city in question. The local chamber office will have a directory listing the addresses and telephone numbers of all other chambers across the country.

What makes an industrial directory so valuable to job-seeking computer drafting technicians is that it contains an alphabetized listing of every industrial company in the host city. Each alphabetized listing contains information of much value to job seekers: company name, mailing address, actual street address, telephone number, contact person, the number of employees, and the products manufactured by the company.

By studying the products manufactured, it can be determined if the company employs drafters. By determining the number of employees, the larger companies, which are the ones most likely to have a computer drafting system, can be identified. Figure 7–3 contains a sample entry from a chamber of commerce industrial directory.

Computer drafting technicians seeking employment in a given city should obtain the industrial directory for that city. By examin-

FIGURE 7-3 Sample industrial directory entry.

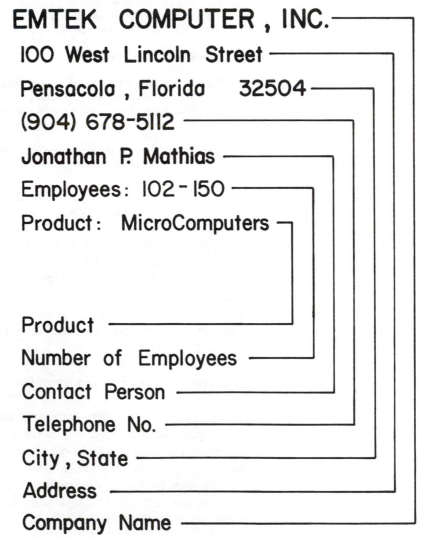

ing its contents carefully, they can make a list of the 20 to 30 most promising potential employers in that city. These are the employers who will then be contacted concerning employment.

Telephone Directories

Another valuable job-seeking tool for any specific city is the telephone directory for that city. The telephone directory, more specifically the classified section of the telephone directory, contains information of much value to the job-seeking computer drafting technician. Drafters seeking jobs in architectural- or engineering-oriented drafting fields will find telephone directories particularly helpful.

The classified section is arranged alphabetically. Drafters seeking employment as computer drafting technicians in the architectural field need only look under "architects" to find an alphabetized listing with addresses and telephone numbers (Figure 7-4). The same is true of engineering-oriented drafting fields.

Drafters who have used chamber of commerce directories or telephone directories to compile lists of potential employers in cities of their choice are now ready to begin making arrangements for contacting them. However, before contacting potential employers, the drafter must write a résumé, prepare a standard letter of inquiry, and develop a list of questions that might be asked during interviews.

52 Architects

Architects (Cont'd)

Coxwell, Allen   AIA

612 North Anderson Street _ _ _ _ _ _ _ _ 873-4121

Jones, Jones, & Assoc. AIA

500 Major Street _ _ _ _ _ _ _ _ _ _ _ _ _ 622-4012

FIGURE 7-4 Sample telephone directory entry.

CONTACTING POTENTIAL EMPLOYERS

Potential employers can be contacted one of three ways: in person, by telephone, or by mail. Regardless of which method is used, it is important to make a positive first impression. The purpose of contacting a potential employer is to arrange a formal interview. One of the best ways of doing this is by mail. Telephone or in-person contacts may come at a bad time for the employer, which is the last thing the job seeker wants. However, mail inquiries have the advantage of allowing employers to study the matter at their own chosen time and to give it more thorough consideration before deciding whether or not to arrange an interview. Employers who respond to mail inquiries are very likely to have a job that they would like to fill.

Letters of Inquiry

A letter of inquiry can be an effective job-seeking tool if properly written. To make sure that a potential employer forms a positive first impression, job-seeking computer drafting technicians should follow several simple rules when preparing a letter of inquiry:

1. Every letter mailed out should be an original. Do not send photocopies of a standard letter.

2. Letters of inquiry should be brief and to the point. Remember, employers are busy people.

3. Keep in mind the four W's when writing a letter of inquiry: who, what, where, and when.

4. Always mail letters of inquiry to a specific person. Never mail letters of inquiry to "Dear Sir" or "To Whom It May Concern."

The letter of inquiry begins with an explanation of who the writer is. The following samples of introductory sentences might be used by job-seeking computer drafting technicians:

Dear Mr. Walker:

I am an architectural computer drafting technician from Fort Walton Beach, Florida.

Dear Mr. Jonsworth:

I am a computer drafting technician in the area of mechanical drafting from Niceville, Florida.

The second sentence tells the employer exactly what the writer wants. This usually takes more than one sentence, but should be accomplished as briefly and succinctly as possible. The following samples of sentences might be used by job-seeking computer drafting technicians:

I plan to relocate to your area as soon as I am able to secure a responsible position of employment in my field. I have examined the job market in the Dallas area and find that my training and career goals mesh well with the employment needs of your drafting department.

I would like to relocate to your area and am seeking employment in my field as a prerequisite to doing so. While examining the job market in Orlando, I discovered that my training and career goals fit well with your company's needs for highly skilled computer drafting technicians.

The next part of the letter of inquiry tells the employer when the writer can be available for an interview or to begin work. It also explains that a résumé has been enclosed along with the letter and that references will be furnished upon request. The following sample sentences might be used by job-seeking computer drafting technicians:

I can be available for an interview or to begin work on July 1, 1983, or anytime thereafter. I have enclosed a résumé and will be happy to furnish references upon request.

I am available for an interview or to begin work immediately. I have enclosed a résumé and will furnish references upon request.

The final part of the letter of inquiry is a simple, but positive closing. The final sentence restates the positive tone of the whole letter and is very important. The following sample sentences might be used by job-seeking computer drafting technicians:

Thank you very much for your consideration; I look forward to receiving your response.

Thank you very much for considering my employment request; I look forward to your decision.

Figures 7–5 and 7–6 are examples of well-written letters of inquiry that might be used by job-seeking computer drafting technicians.

The Résumé

A résumé is a one- or two-page summary of a person's qualifications in a particular field. Together with the letter of inquiry, it is mailed or delivered to prospective employers as a key element in the job search. The purpose of a résumé is to sell a potential employer on one's qualifications in hopes of being invited to a job interview. A well-prepared résumé is an important ingredient in the job search. For this reason, it is important that computer drafting technicians be able to develop a well-written, concise, but impressive résumé.

A résumé consists of several different components, presented in the following order: personal data, career goal, education summary, work experience summary, awards and special notes, and hobbies. Each of these components represents an independent, but vital part of a completed résumé.

Personal data

Personal data contained in a résumé include full name, mailing address, and telephone number. The job-seeking computer drafting technician need not include such information as sex, race, marital status, age, or number of children. Some high-level management

```
Mr. James R. Andrews
Chief Drafter
BOYD BROTHERS MANUFACTURING COMPANY
1001 Arabian Parkway
Samford, Florida 32579                              October 6, 1982

Dear Mr. Andrews:

I am a mechanical drafter with special training in computer aided drafting.
I would like to relocate to the Samford area as soon as I am able to locate
a responsible position in my field.

I have examined the employment opportunities in Samford and find that I
would like to work for Boyd Brothers Manufacturing Company.  My mechanical
drafting background coupled with my computer aided drafting training seems
to mesh well with the employment needs of your drafting department.

I would appreciate an interview at your earliest convenience.  A resume of
my qualifications is attached.  I will be happy to furnish references and
samples of my work upon request.

Thank you very much.  I look forward to hearing from you.


Sincerely,



Ronald J. Morgan
Mechanical Drafter and
CAD Specialist
```

FIGURE 7-5   Sample letter of inquiry.

positions call for this type of information on a résumé, but not computer drafting technician positions. It should be remembered that brevity is the key to a good résumé. The primary reason for listing personal data is so that employers will have the information they need for contacting applicants to set up an interview. Several points are important to ensure that a résumé stands out in a crowd — and this is important, because most job openings attract more than one applicant. The first point is to list the complete name (first, middle, last) with all letters capitalized. For example: MARY JANE ANDERSON or ANDREW FORD LEONA. This will call attention to the name. The second point is to list a complete mailing address, including the zip code, without abbreviations. Abbreviating words in a résumé will cause it to appear hurriedly done. The final point is to give both a work and a home telephone number and include area codes for both. The following examples show how job-seeking computer drafting technicians might list the personal data on a résumé:

```
Ritter M. MacMillan, AIA
MacMillan and MacMillan, Architects
5 Business Park Plaza
Valparaiso, Florida  32683                    October 10, 1982

Dear Mr. MacMillan:

I recently graduated from Lacy C. Elmore Technical Center with an Associates
Degree in Architectural Drafting.  I am now in the process of seeking em-
ployment in my field.

My training covered residential and commercial design, planning, and drawing.
In addition, I have special training in computer aided drafting.  I am able
to perform all normal architectural drafting tasks on the Auto Trol AD 380
computer aided drafting system.

I am willing to relocate to the Valparaiso area and can be available for an
interview or to begin work immediately.  I have enclosed a resume which ex-
plains my qualifications in more detail.  I will be happy to provide samples
of my work and references during the interview.

Thank you very much for considering my request for an interview.  I look for-
ward to hearing from you.


Sincerely,



John Kenneth Brombaugh
Architectural/Computer Aided Drafter
```

FIGURE 7-6   Sample letter of inquiry.

SAMUEL ALEXANDER BROWN
202 Hudson Circle, Floodville, Arkansas 32568
(904) 432-7412 H
(904) 561-8902 W

MELISSA JANE COX
49603 Booth Avenue
Cantonment, Florida 32504
(904) 968-9403 H
(904) 678-5153 W

Career goal

The career goal is the second component of a résumé and it is
an important component. The career goal tells the employer several
things: (1) that the applicant has chosen a definite career field, has
prepared for that career field, and intends to work in that field; (2)

that the applicant is looking for a particular position rather than just any job; and (3) that the applicant intends to begin work at a productive level and advance according to his or her performance on the job.

Employers want to hire workers who have direction, purpose, and goals. A career goal conveys this type of attitude to employers. However, job-seeking computer drafting technicians should be careful to make sure that their career goal is not written in such a way that it becomes too limited. The ideal career goal is specific enough to show that the applicant has direction within a chosen field, but broad enough to encompass a number of jobs within that field.

Career goals will vary in their wording according to the ambitions of the writer. However, all career goals should contain three basic elements: (1) a stated desire to begin work at a productive level; (2) a stated desire to apply one's knowledge, skills, and training; and (3) a stated desire to advance at a rate equal to one's performance on the job. Employers will form a positive first impression of any applicant whose career goal contains these three elements.

Several sample career goals that might be used by job-seeking computer drafting technicians follow:

> To begin work at a productive level as a computer drafting technician and to advance to a supervisory level at a rate that is commensurate with my performance on the job.

> To begin work at a productive level as a computer drafting technician in the field of architectural drafting and to advance to a designer position at a rate equal to my performance on the job.

> To begin work at a productive level as a computer drafting technician in the field of electronics drafting and to advance to a position as a printed-circuit-board designer at a rate equal to my performance on the job.

Education summary

This component of the résumé is included to give potential employers a brief synopsis of the applicant's educational preparation for the job in question. The phrase "job in question" is significant here. Employers computer drafting technicians want to know what specific educational preparation they have had in the field. A long list of nonrelated education in other fields will serve no purpose. In keeping with the rule of brevity, only the educational preparation that pertains to the job in question should be given an in-depth explanation. Other educational experiences may be listed briefly or omitted altogether.

The education summary in a job-seeking computer drafting technician's résumé contains three basic elements: (1) degree, diploma, or certificate earned and the date it was awarded; (2) school or institution that provided the education; and (3) a comprehensive, but brief summary of what the education covered. Several sample education summaries that might be used by job-seeking computer drafting technicians follow:

ASSOCIATE OF SCIENCE DEGREE. Architectural Drafting and Design. Rockwell Community College, Pensacola, Florida, June 1982.

My architectural drafting training at Rockwell Community College covered math through trigonometry, residential design and drawing, light commercial design and drawing, commercial design and drawing, construction materials and processes, cost estimation, and computer design and drafting. I can operate the Auto-trol AD 380 computer drafting system.

VOCATIONAL CERTIFICATE. Electronics Drafting and Design. Leesburg Area Vocational-Technical School, Fort Walton Beach, Florida, December 1981.

My electronics drafting training at Leesburg Vocational-Technical School covered schematic drawings, connection diagrams, block diagrams, logic design and diagrams, printed-circuit-board design and drawings, chassis drawings, and computer-aided drafting and design. I can operate the Tektronix 3054 computer drafting system.

VOCATIONAL DIPLOMA. Mechanical Drafting and Design. Niceville Technical High School, June 1983.

My mechanical drafting training at Niceville Technical High School covered product design and working drawings, jig and fixture design and working drawings, tool and die design and drawings, manufacturing processes, geometric dimensioning and tolerancing, computer-aided manufacturing, and computer-aided design and drafting. I can operate the ComputerVision computer drafting system.

Work experience summary

Most information on résumé writing is geared toward the person with work experience. For this reason, a great deal of time is spent explaining how to list all pertinent experience in reverse chronological order. However, this type of information serves little or no purpose for the typical drafting student. Most drafting students have no work experience in their field. Many have no work experience at all.

It is important to be able to list some type of work experience on a résumé. The more closely the experience relates to the drafting field in question the better. However, listing totally unrelated or even volunteer work is better than listing nothing. Employers are reluctant to hire people who have never worked for fear that they will not have formed good working habits, such as punctuality, dependability, and seeing a task through from beginning to end.

The following sample work experience summaries might be used by job-seeking computer drafting technicians:

BLUEPRINT CLERK AND ERRAND BOY. Ricks-Jones-Smith Architects. Pensacola, Florida. January 1981–August 1982.

My duties with Ricks-Jones-Smith included printing, folding, stamping, and mailing approved drawings; distributing interoffice mail; pickup and delivery; and maintenance of a GAF 390 ammonia developing print machine.

SALESCLERK. Devonshire Boutique. Fort Walton Beach, Florida. April 1982–September 1982.

My duties with Devonshire Boutique included waiting on customers, rehanging and displaying outfits that had been tried on, writing up sales slips, cashiering, and stocking.

SUNSHINE VOLUNTEER. Smithboro Hospital, Crestview, Florida. June 1982–August 1982 and June 1983–August 1983.

My work as a sunshine volunteer included playing games with patients, walking patients, talking with patients, pushing wheel-chaired people to and from the cafeteria, and housekeeping duties.

Occasionally, a drafting student will have actual work experience in drafting. When this is the case, that experience should be listed first and explained in depth. A good rule of thumb in preparing the work experience summary for a résumé is to list those experiences which most relate to the job in question first and those which least relate last.

Awards and special note

Although awards received probably have little bearing, if any, on how qualified a person is for a given job, they should be included on a résumé. So should any other miscellaneous items of note. It should be remembered that employers are people and that the purpose of a résumé is to create enough interest to have an interview granted. An award or some special notation might just be the little extra that causes a potential to grant an interview.

The following sample awards and special note entries might be found on the résumés of job-seeking computer drafting technicians:

First Place Winner. Fourth Annual Drafting and Design Contest. Okaloosa-Walton Junior College, December 1980.

Chosen for entry in "Who's Who in American Community Colleges" for 1981.

Made Dean's List with 3.76 grade-point average on a 4.0 scale during the fall, winter, and spring semesters of 1981.

Senior Class President. Niceville Vocational-Technical High School, Class of 1981.

Outstanding Drafting and Design Student of the Year for 1981. Carlsbad Vocational-Technical School, Carlsbad, Florida.

Hobbies

This category, like the preceding one, is included to appeal to the personal side of employers. Some employers are very interested in the hobbies and outside activities of potential employees, whereas others will hardly glance at this section of the résumé. However, in order to leave no stone unturned in an attempt to gain an interview, it is best to include hobbies. This ensures that if the employer is one of those who is interested, the information he or she is seeking will be available. If the employer is not interested in the hobbies of an applicant, he or she will simply ignore them.

Hobbies should be the shortest segment of the résumé. Hobbies are simply listed. No detailed information is required, nor should any be offered. The following entries are samples of hobbies that might be listed on a job-seeking computer drafting technicians résumé:

Tennis, golf, and racquetball

Hunting, fishing, and mountain climbing

Square dancing and reading

References

References are usually supplied by letter or telephone and are not a part of the résumé. However, on occasion a reference or references can be included on the résumé if extra content is needed to complete a full page. Sample reference entries that might be found on the résumé of a job-seeking computer drafting technician follow:

Dr. Ned C. Jones
Chairman
Drafting and Design Department
Niceville Community College
101 College Boulevard
Niceville, Florida 32578
(904) 678-1552 Ext. 372

Mr. James A. Smith
Drafting Instructor
Pensacola Technical High School
1559 North Palafox Street
Pensacola, Florida 32501
(904) 432-7412 Ext 654

Ms. Freda J. Paine
Chief Drafter
Diversified Technical Services Company
211 Hudson Circle
Niceville, Florida 32578
(904) 678-4040

Figures 7-7 through 7-11 present samples of résumés for various computer drafting fields.

The Interview

The interview is the most critical step in the job-seeking process. Everything that preceded the interview was done for the purpose of gaining an interview. The interview is undertaken for the pur-

FIGURE 7-7   Mechanical drafter's résumé.

```
                         SAMUEL ALEXANDER BROWN
              202 Hudson Circle, Floodville, Arkansas  32568
                             (904) 432-7412 H
                             (904) 561-8902 W


                                CAREER GOAL

    To begin work at a productive level as a computer drafting technician in
    a mechanical drafting position which will allow me to advance to a super-
    visory level at a rate that is commensurate with my performance on the
    job.


                              EDUCATION SUMMARY

    ASSOCIATE OF SCIENCE DEGREE.  Mechanical Drafting Technology.  Niceville
         Community College, Niceville, Florida, August 1981

    My mechanical drafting training at Niceville Community College covered
    product design and working drawings, jig and fixture design and working
    drawings, tool and die design and drawings, manufacturing processes, geo-
    metric dimensioning and tolerancing, computer aided drafting and computer
    aided manufacturing.  I can operate the Auto-Trol AD 380 computer draft-
    ing system.


                           WORK EXPERIENCE SUMMARY

    BLUEPRINT CLERK AND ERRAND RUNNER.  Longfield Manufacturing Company,
         Crestview, Florida, January 1981 - August 1981.

    My duties at Longfield Manufacturing Company included collecting and dis-
    tributing interoffice mail, inventorying the drafting supplies once each
    week and reporting those items which needed to be ordered, running prints,
    filing original drawings, stacking check prints for the jobs in progress, and
    collecting the mail from the post office once each day.


                            AWARDS AND SPECIAL NOTE

    FIRST PLACE WINNER.  Mechanical Drafting Division.  Tenth Annual Niceville
         Community College Drafting Contest.  May 1981

    DEAN'S LIST.  Fall, Winter, Summer Semesters of 1980-81 school year with
         a 3.56 grade point average on a 4.00 scale.

    PRESIDENT.  Niceville Community College Drafting and Design Club for 1980-
         81 school year.


                                  HOBBIES

    Long distance running, tennis, and snow skiing.  I participate in competi-
    tive long distance runs and marathons.
```

pose of gaining a job. It is important for job-seeking computer drafting technicians to be well prepared for interviews. What follows is a list of "do's" and "dont's" that job seekers should be aware of in preparing for an interview:

Do's

1. Make sure that you are well groomed and properly dressed for the interview.

2. Visit the restroom before an interview to avoid the embarrassment of having to interrupt an interview for that purpose.

3. Be pleasant but businesslike. Use a firm but not overbearing handshake and look the interviewer squarely in the eyes.

FIGURE 7-8 Architectural drafter's résumé.

```
                    JANICE RITA CLAYTON
                 6116 Avenue of South Smithville
                    Crestview, Florida  32561
                       (904) 682-2400 H


                         CAREER GOAL

To begin work at a productive level as a computer drafting technician in
an architectural drafting position which will allow me to advance to a de-
signer's position at a rate that is in line with my performance on the job.


                       EDUCATION SUMMARY

OCCUPATIONAL CERTIFICATE.  Architectural Drafting and Design.  Fort Wal-
    ton Beach Area Vocational-Technical Center.  June 1982

My architectural drafting training at Fort Walton Beach Area Vocational-
Technical Center covered residential design and planning, construction of
residential house plans according to VA/FHA specifications, preparation
of architectural drawings for commercial buildings, materials take-offs
for construction cost estimation, pin registered overlay drafting, team
drafting, scissors drafting, and computer aided drafting.  I can operate
the Tektronix 3054 computer drafting system.


                     WORK EXPERIENCE SUMMARY

LIBRARIAN'S ASSISTANT (Part-time).  Fort Walton Beach Public Library,
    Fort Walton Beach, Florida.  September 1982 - Present.

My duties at the Fort Walton Beach Public Library included checkout and
checkin of books, returning books to the shelves, processing payment of
overdue fines, processing and displaying weekly and monthly periodicals,
and supervision of the children's section of the library.


                      AWARDS AND SPECIAL NOTE

MEMBER OF THE YEAR FOR 1982.  Fort Walton Beach Sunshine Club.

BILLY BOWLEGS RACQUETBALL TOURNAMENT CHAMPION.  Girls Division's, 16 to
    18 year old division.


                           HOBBIES

Racquetball, tennis, biking, and outdoor recreation activities such as
camping and snorkeling.
```

```
                        PETER BROOKS MAJORS
                      604 Booth Avenue, Apartment 17
                       Valparaiso, Florida  32568
                           (904) 862-2921 H

                              CAREER GOAL

To begin work at a productive level in a civil engineering related draft-
ing position which will allow me to advance to a position of computer
drafting technician at a rate that is in line with my performance on the
job.

                           EDUCATION SUMMARY

DIPLOMA.  Freeport Technical High School.  Area of emphasis - Civil
     Drafting, June 1982.

My studies at Freeport Technical High School covered the typical high
school curriculum with special emphasis on civil drafting.  Drafting
topics studied included:  single property plats, multiple lot plats
(subdivisions), writing metes and bounds property descriptions from
field notes, complete traverse computations, acreage calculations, co-
ordinate plotting, latitude and departure calculations, closure calc-
ulations, and cut and fill problems.  I can plot single and multiple lot
plats on the Keuffel and Esser IGS/330 Interactive Graphic System.

                        WORK EXPERIENCE SUMMARY

VOLUNTEER OFFICE ASSISTANT.  Drafting Department, Freeport Technical
     High School.  1981/82 school year.

My duties in the Drafting Department of Freeport Technical High School
included collecting and cleaning all inking equipment at the end of each
day, supervising beginning students on the operation of the IGS/330
computer drafting system.

                        AWARDS AND SPECIAL NOTE

Silver Medalist.  Annual Fort Walton Beach Invitation Swimming Meet.

                                HOBBIES

Swimming and sailing.  I swim in competitive swimming meets and sailing
regattas.

                              REFERENCE

                         Mr. Andrew Spere
                         Drafting Instructor
                      Freeport Technical High School
                           (904) 862-2111
```

FIGURE 7-9   Civil drafter's résumé.

4. Make sure that you know the interviewer's name and position.

5. Always take money to an interview — no, not to bribe the employer — you never know when a potential employer might ask you to lunch.

6. Scout out the potential place of employment prior to an interview when possible.

7. Learn as much about a company as possible before an interview.

8. Let the interviewer set the pace of the interview and decide when the interview is over.

9. Make sure that the last question that you ask in an interview is when the employer will notify you of his or her decision.

```
                              DAVID LEE CONNORS
                           1776 East Nine Mile Road
                           Pensacola, Florida 32504
                              (904) 476-6121 H
                              (904) 477-7300 W


                                  CAREER GOAL

        To begin work at a productive level as a computer drafting technician
        in a process piping drafting position that will allow me to advance to a
        designer position at a rate in line with my performance on the job


                               EDUCATION SUMMARY

        ASSOCIATE OF APPLIED SCIENCE DEGREE  Pensacola Junior College, Pensacola,
             Florida, December 1981.

        My studies at Pensacola Junior College provided an in-depth treatment of
        process piping drafting with special emphasis on computer aided drafting.
        Topics covered include nomenclature, plans, and details, piping plans,
        isometric pictorials, flow diagrams, and specifications.


                             WORK EXPERIENCE SUMMARY

        WAITER.  Antoine's Fine Foods Restaurant.  Pensacola, Florida,  September
             1980 to present.


                             AWARDS AND SPECIAL NOTE

        DRAFTING CLUB PRESIDENT.  Pensacola Junior College, 1980/81 school year.

        Student member of the American Institute for Design and Drafting, 1980/81.


                                    HOBBIES

        Spectator sports such as football, baseball, basketball, and boxing.


                                  REFERENCES

        Dr. Salem F. Abercrombie               Mr. Clement C. Atlee
        Chairman                               Drafting Instructor
        Drafting and Design Department         Pensacola Junior College
        Pensacola Junior College               College Blvd
        College Blvd                           Pensacola, Florida  32501
        Pensacola, Florida  32501              (904) 456-1000 Ext 456
        (904) 456-1000 Ext 376
```

FIGURE 7-10   Piping drafter's résumé.

Dont's

1. Don't be late to an interview. Show up 10 to 15 minutes early.

2. Don't go into an interview with candy, gum, or breath mints in your mouth.

3. Don't slouch, fidgit, or lean on the interviewer's desk. Sit up in a comfortable, but erect manner.

4. Don't call attention to your nervousness by rattling change in your pocket, cracking your knuckles, or drumming your fingers on the desk.

5. Don't tell jokes or make wisecracks.

6. Don't go overboard with "sir" and "maam." Be respectful, but remember it's an interview, not Marine Corps boot camp.

```
                          DEBORAH MARIE SCHULZE
                       109 Robinwood Drive, Northwest
                       Fort Walton Beach, Florida 32548
                               (904) 243-1288 H
                               (904) 678-4040 W


                                  CAREER GOAL

        To begin work at a productive level as a computer drafting technician in
        an electronics drafting position that will allow me to apply my training
        and experience and advance to a supervisory level at a rate commensurate
        with my performance on the job.


                               EDUCATION SUMMARY

        ASSOCIATE OF SCIENCE DEGREE and ASSOCIATE OF ARTS DEGREE.  Okaloosa-
           Walton Junior College, Niceville, Florida, December 1980.

        My studies at Okaloosa-Walton Junior College covered all phases of draft-
        ing and design with special, in-depth emphasis on electronics drafting.
        Major areas of study included schematic drawings, wiring diagrams, logic
        diagrams, chassis drawings, and printed circuit board design, layout, and
        tape up.


                            WORK EXPERIENCE SUMMARY

        ELECTRONICS DRAFTER.  Diversified Technical Services Company, Niceville,
           Florida.  January 1980 - Present.

        My duties at Diversified Technical Services Company included laying out wir-
        ing diagrams for government defense contracts and printed circuit board de-
        sign, layout, and tape up for civilian contracts.  I am qualified in the
        use of the ComputerVision Company's computer drafting system.


                             AWARDS AND SPECIAL NOTE

        OWJC SINGLES TENNIS CHAMPION.  1979.

        Formula Vee Junior Division Race Winner.  Bainbridge, Georgia, 1979.

        DEANS LIST.  1979/80 school year.  Okaloosa-Walton Junior College.

        CONTEST WINNER.  Fourth Annual OWJC Drafting and Design Contest, 1980.


                                    HOBBIES

        Sailing, race car driving, tennis, biking, camping, and hiking.  I like
        all outdoor recreational activities.
```

FIGURE 7-11 Electronics drafter's résumé.

7. Don't give simple yes or no answers. Expound on your answers, but do not become verbose.

8. Don't be boastful.

9. Don't interrupt the interviewer.

10. Don't lose your composure if you trip over a difficult question.

11. Don't constantly look at your watch during the interview.

12. Don't appear timid. Be confident, but not cocky.

The job-seeking computer drafting technician should be prepared to answer specific questions about drafting and computer-aided drafting. Having completed the chapters in this textbook, technical questions should pose no problem to the job-seeking computer drafting technician. However, other types of questions are also subject to come up in a job interview that do not relate to the applicant's technical skills. These questions can be as important as the technical questions. The following list of questions are samples of those which might be asked of job-seeking computer drafting technicians about subjects other than their technical training:

Frequently asked interview questions

1. Why did you decide to go into drafting?
2. What are your long-term goals as a computer drafting technician?
3. Why did you decide you would like to work for this company?
4. Explain your technical training and how it prepared you for this job.
5. Are you willing to spend time as a drafting trainee?
6. Are you willing to relocate to another company within our chain?
7. Why should I hire you for this job?
8. What do you like to do when you are not working?
9. How do you feel about continuing your education?
10. What is the lowest salary you will accept to begin this job?

KEEPING A JOB AND ADVANCING IN IT

For the inexperienced job seeker, finding a job can be a job in itself. In addition, once a job has been secured, the work does not stop. It took a certain amount of technical skills to get a job. It will take "employability skills" to keep a job and advance in it. Employability skills are those nontechnical skills that make a person a valuable employee regardless of the job. Figure 7–12 contains a list of important employability skills with which the job seeker should be familiar.

In addition to the employability skills explained in Figure 7–12, computer drafting technicians, to advance in their career field, must also be lifelong learners willing to continuously update their knowledge and skills. There is no occupation in which the knowledge and skills required are static, and drafting is no exception.

There is no such thing as learning everything there is to know about a certain occupation and ceasing to learn. The knowledge and skills required to practice a highly technical occupation such as drafting are in a constant state of flux. Computer-aided drafting is the perfect example of this phenomenon.

If a computer drafting technician plans to make a career of the field, he or she must be committed to an occupational lifetime of constant learning and change. Drafting, at one time, was done on lap boards with T-squares. Then came drafting tables and parallel bars. These were followed by drafting machines and hundreds of different types of templates. After this there was scissors drafting, team drafting, and pen registered overlay drafting. Now there is computer-aided drafting. All of these innovations have occurred during the occupational life span of many drafters who still work in the field.

EMPLOYABILITY SKILLS

1. BE DEPENDABLE. Come to work on time and work while you are there. An employer needs to know that you can be counted on to be there when needed and to be working without a need for close supervision.

2. BE A LIFELONG LEARNER. The knowledge and skills that you developed in school were enough to get you a job. However, to keep a job and advance in it, you will have to continue learning on the job throughout your career.

3. BE A WORKER. Avoid joining the water cooler clique, coffee pot gang, or the all-day clock watchers. Everyone needs a break while working and you will, too. However, do not get into the habit of overdoing it. Breaks are justifiable only when they improve your productivity.

4. BE SELF-SUFFICIENT. Nothing is wrong with asking questions; in fact, it is to be encouraged. However, before asking a question, be sure that you have made an effort to find the answer for yourself.

5. CONSTANTLY IMPROVE. Make a concerted effort to improve your work every day. Do not be afraid to attempt new projects that deal with things you have not yet confronted. This is the best way to make sure that you continue to learn and improve every day.

6. BE PERSONABLE. Getting along with fellow workers will be very important. Many drafting tasks are performed by teams of drafters working together, so the ability to get along with people is a must.

FIGURE 7-12 Employability skills.

SUMMARY AND REVIEW

- Job-seeking computer drafting technicians must be willing to relocate for employment if they hope to find a good job in their field.

- Job-seeking computer drafting technicians must learn to market their skills effectively before beginning the job search. This means learning to write letters of inquiry, a résumé, an interview, and identifying potential employers.

- Job-seeking computer drafting technicians must be willing to start at the bottom in their field and work up.

- Job-seeking computer drafting technicians should be positive and assertive during their job search.

- Job-seeking computer drafting technicians should avoid becoming frustrated during the job search.

- Before relocating to any other city for employment, job-seeking computer drafting technicians should investigate such things as taxes, housing, transportation, continuing education opportunities, and other personal considerations.

- Two valuable aids for locating potential employers in a given city are Chambers of Commerce Industry Directories and the Yellow Pages of telephone directories.

- Job-seeking computer drafting technicians should be able to write an attractive letter of inquiry that covers the four W's: who, what, when, and where.

- Letters of inquiry should always be original letters, never photo-copies of a master letter.

- Letters of inquiry should be brief and to the point.

- Letters of inquiry should be mailed to specific people, never to "Dear Sir" or "To Whom It May Concern."

- A résumé is a one- or two-page summary of a person's qualifications in a particular career field.

- A typical résumé consists of personal data, a career goal, an education summary, a work experience summary, a list of awards or items of special note, and a list of hobbies.

- The interview is the most critical step in the job-seeking process; therefore, job-seeking computer drafting technicians should be well prepared for the interview.

- In an interview, it is important to show up on time, be properly dressed, be pleasant but businesslike, use a firm, but not overbearing handshake, and let the interviewer set the pace.

- The job-seeking computer drafting technician should be prepared to answer a number of questions during an interview that do not relate to his or her technical training, such as: "Why do you want to work for this company?"

- Once a job has been secured, keeping it and advancing in it will require employability skills, which include being dependable, being a learner, being a worker, being self-sufficient, being personable, and always striving to improve.

- Computer drafting technicians must continue to learn on the job for the entire length of their career.

SELF-TEST Directions

Respond to each question without referring to the chapter. Once you have completed the test, refer to the chapter to check your answers. Reread any portion of the chapter covering questions you miss before proceeding to the next chapter.

1. Indicate whether each of the following statements is true or false.
   a. The job seeker who is willing to relocate for employment will usually stand a better chance of getting a good job.
   b. Letters of inquiry should be typed, signed, and then photocopied as many times as necessary.
   c. The proper way to begin a letter of inquiry sent to a potential employer is "Dear Sir or Madam."

2. Define the term "résumé."

3. Explain what "learning to market your skills" means.

4. List three of the five "job seeker's commandments."

5. It is important for a job-seeking computer drafting technician to investigate any city to which he or she might relocate for employment. List three things that should be considered about a city.

6. Name two valuable aids the job-seeking computer drafting technician can use to identify potential employers in a given city.

7. A typical résumé contains six major components. What are they?

8. What three things should a computer drafting technician keep in mind when going into an interview?

9. Computer drafting technicians are able to get jobs because of their technical skills. However, to keep a job and advance in it, they must also have employability skills. Name six employability skills.

10. Complete the text of the following letter of inquiry as if you are the job seeker.

```
Mr. Charles A. Alexander
Chief Drafter
Computer Drafting Section
Diversified Technical Products Company, Inc.
100 Industrial Park Circle
Atland, Florida  32546

Dear Mr. Alexander:




















Sincerely,


Donald C. Larsen
Computer Drafting Technician
```

11. Complete the following résumé as if you were the job seeker.

```
                            Donald C. Larsen
                211 Hudson Circle, Niceville, Florida  32578
                            (904) 678-4142

                              Career Goal




                           Education Summary




                         Work Experience Summary




                          Awards or Special Note




                                Hobbies
```

GLOSSARY

Accessories Sometimes called peripheral equipment. Items of hardware that enhance the capability of a computer or computer drafting system. Printers, plotters, and hard-copy units are all accessories.

Access time The amount of time that elapses between when a computer receives an instruction to place data in storage or call data up from storage and when the data actually begin to move in either direction.

Alphanumeric Alphabetical and numerical characters, such as A, S, T, Y, U, H, 1, 5, 7, 8, etc.

Analog Uses a continuous physical quantity such as voltage to represent a numerical value.

Annotation The process of entering text on a drawing. This is the computer-aided drafting version of what is called "lettering" in manual drafting.

Automatic dimensioning The computer actually performs all the various dimensioning tasks automatically. This includes measuring and computing distances, drawing dimension lines, extension lines, and arrowheads as needed.

BASIC "Beginner's All-Purpose Symbolic Instruction Code." A simple computer programming language that is easy to learn and very popular. It was invented at Dartmouth College in 1963.

Benchmarks A set of standards used to test a computer system, an individual piece of hardware, or new software. Benchmarks determine if the subject is working properly or according to specifications.

Binary A system in which all data are represented by one of two signals or a numbering system in which all numbers are represented by one or a combination of two digits, 0 and 1. Binary numbers are the numbers of computer math.

BOM An acronym for the phrase "bill of materials." A BOM is a list of all the materials required to complete the manufacture of a product or a project. They are an integral part of structural and architectural drafting.

Bug A flaw or error in the design of a program.

CAD This is an acronym that originated for the phrase "computer-aided design." It has also come to be used for "computer-aided drafting." To distinguish between the two, purists insist that CAD be used for the design aspect and that AD (automated drafting) be used for the drafting aspect. However, since the computer figures so directly in the process of converting from manual to automated drafting, computer-aided drafting has caught on and seems destined to become rooted in the language.

Central processing unit Usually called the CPU, it is the brain center of the computer system. The CPU actually directs all the other components in a system. It contains a control section and a logic section.

Chip An extremely small piece of material usually made of silicon that carries the elements of an electronic circuit. In spite of the fact that a chip may be smaller than a person's fingernail, it can carry thousands of electronic components.

Cross hairs A horizontal plane intersected at 90 degrees by a vertical plane. Used on a cursor to indicate a point that is to be digitized or displayed.

Crosshatching Process of filling in an outline with a series of angled lines to highlight a part of a drawing or to indicate a section that has been cut and is being displayed.

CRT Short for "cathode ray tube," which is a television-like display.

Cursor An instrument used manually to indicate the point of action, a symbol to be digitized, a point to be digitized, and so on. If a sketch were to be entered into the computer and displayed on the CRT screen, a cursor could be used to trace the sketch manually, allowing it to be digitized.

Database A comprehensive collection of data having predetermined structure and organization suitable for various uses in a computer-aided drafting system. Symbols represented on a menu are part of the system's database.

Debug Identifying, locating, and correcting mistakes in a program or malfunctions in a computer-aided drafting system.

Digitizing The process of converting graphical data into computer-usable electrical signals. Digitizing is accomplished with an electronic pen or a cursor and a digitizing tablet or table.

Disk A flat, donut-shaped device on which information is stored. Disk storage in computer-aided drafting replaces filing drawers used in manual drafting for storing drawings.

Graphical data Geometric shapes such as circles, arcs, curves, planes, lines, and polygons which make up drawings.

Grid A network of uniformly spaced points, such as those on graph paper, which can be used for locating the positions of data displayed on the CRT or plotted.

Hard copy An actual copy of anything that can be displayed on the CRT screen (i.e., photocopy, printout, original drawing, program documentation, etc.).

Hardware The physical components of a computer-aided drafting system, such as the CRT, CPU, plotter, printer, and digitizer.

Input The process through which data are entered into a computer-aided drafting system or the actual data entered into the system.

Input/output device Any hardware component that can be used both for entering data in or removing data from a computer-aided drafting system. The most frequently used input/output device is the CRT.

Intelligent terminal A terminal with its own processing power. An intelligent terminal can still process data when the central system is shut down.

Interactive graphics Ability to perform graphic operations directly on a system and have immediate feedback. An example is the ability to digitize a sketch and have it immediately displayed on the CRT screen.

Joystick An input device that allows the operator to plot X-Y-Z points directly on the CRT screen without the digitizing process.

Memory Any form of data storage used in a computer system. There is the general purpose storage of the computer and various types of auxiliary storage.

Menu An input device that consists of a sheet of symbols overlayed on a digitizing surface. It allows symbols to be entered whole rather than created from scratch. Menus serve the same purpose in computer-aided drafting that templates serve in manual drafting.

Mirroring A drawing capability on a computer-aided drafting system which allows the system to provide mirror images of symmetrical objects. It is a timesaving strategy for inputting graphical data. For example, when entering a symmetrical object into the system, the drafter may enter one half of the object and create the other half with the mirror function.

Off-line Hardware in a system but not directly under the control of the system.

On-line Hardware in a system connected directly to and under the control of the system.

Peripheral device A hardware device that can be used in a computer system for inputting and outputting data.

Plotter The hardware device used for making original drawings of data displayed on the CRT screen.

Program A set of instructions written in a computer language designed to cause a computer to perform a certain task.

Repaint Automatically redrawing a display image on a CRT screen to give a picture that is free of digitizing indicators, attention points, deleted data, and so on.

Rotation Turning of an object about a point or axis to gain views of the object from various angles.

Rubber banding An input technique for creating lines in which the line being made has one end fixed and the other following a command.

Software All the programs, rules, and documentation that allow the operation of a computer system.

Storage Entering data into a device and holding them there until they are needed again.

Tablet A digitizing tablet used for inputting graphical data in coordinate form.

Terminal An input/output device made up of a CRT and a keyboard. This is the hardware item used most by computer-aided drafting system operators and users.

Window A bounded area within a CRT screen that contains a portion of whatever image is being displayed.

Zoom To enlarge or decrease the size of the images being displayed on the CRT screen.

Appendix

COMPUTER-AIDED DRAFTING EXERCISES

The exercises contained in this appendix are for students in drafting programs that have a computer-aided drafting system available. The problems are designed to allow students to develop basic skills in using computer-aided drafting hardware to perform drafting tasks which they have traditionally performed manually.

The exercises contained in this appendix are of a general nature and may be performed on most computer-aided drafting systems without requiring special hardware. Once a student has completed all the exercises, he or she is ready to use the computer-aided drafting system in place of manual techniques for completing the assignments provided by the instructor.

Instructors may wish to alter the directions for exercises to make them correspond with their individual teaching plans or to make them more compatible with the computer-aided drafting hardware available in their programs.

The exercises in this appendix are all at the basic level. Instructors are encouraged to add assignments of their own once students have completed these, so as to advance their development even further.

Problem 1: Lettering Exercise

Begin developing keyboard skills for entering alphanumeric data by entering the following paragraph into your computer-aided drafting system:

Computer-aided drafting is the latest innovation in a long list of technological advances designed to make the drafter more productive. Although there have been many other such advances brought about for the purpose of facilitating more work in less time, computer-aided drafting represents the most dramatic development in the history of the occupation. All other advances have simply been ways to improve on the manual techniques used for performing most drafting tasks. Computer-aided drafting represents a total departure from manual techniques. Drafters are now able to make use of automated techniques in performing their everyday duties on the job.

Problem 2: Linework Exercise

Begin developing linework skills by recreating the geometric shapes contained in Figure A-1 on your computer-aided drafting system. You may use the keyboard, a menu, and/or digitizing unit. The first step is to create a full-scale sketch of Figure A-1 on graph paper.

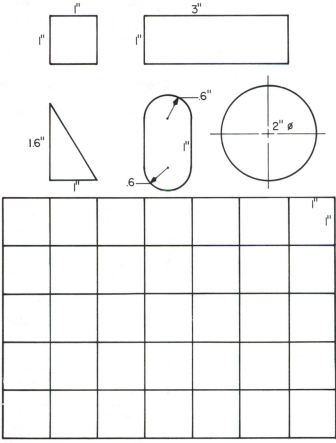

FIGURE A-1

Problem 3: Dimensioning Exercise

Make a full-scale sketch of the object in Figure A-2. Digitize the sketch and display it on the CRT screen. Using the coordinates provided, compute the dimensions for the object. Input the dimensions manually using the keyboard and menu.

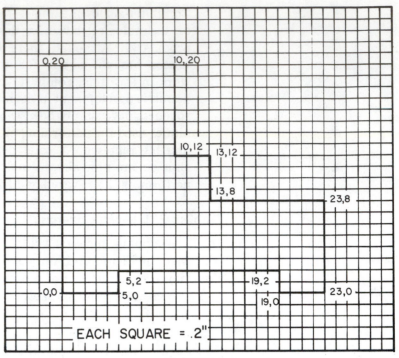

FIGURE A-2

Problem 4: Crosshatching Exercise

Make a full-scale sketch of the object in Figure A-3. Digitize the sketch and display it on the CRT screen. Crosshatch the entire object with any style of crosshatching line contained in your computer-aided drafting system's database.

FIGURE A-3

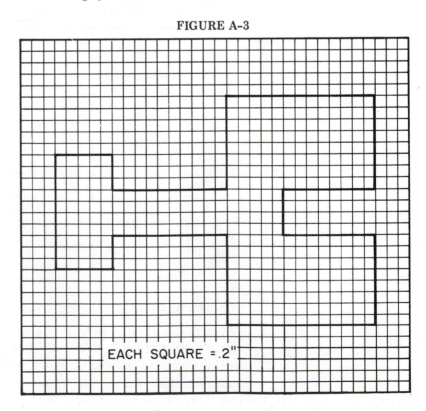

Problem 5: Drawing Manipulation Exercise

Make a full-scale sketch of the object in Figure A-4. Digitize the sketch and display it on the CRT screen. Rotate the object into three different positions and plot an original drawing of each position.

Problem 6: Scaling Exercise

Make a full-scale sketch of the object in Figure A-5. Digitize the sketch and display it on the CRT screen. Perform the following scaling exercises: (1) Command the plotter to plot an original drawing of the object in a drafting area which is A size or smaller; (2) Command the plotter to plot the object half-size in a drafting area that is B size.

Problem 7: Advanced Digitizing Exercise

Manually redraw the floor plan in Figure A-6 to a scale of $\frac{1}{4}$ inch = 1 foot. Digitize the drawing and display it on the CRT screen. Input all room designations, dimensions, and notes. Command the plotter to create an original drawing of the floor plan in a drafting area that is 8 × 10 inches.

FIGURE A-4

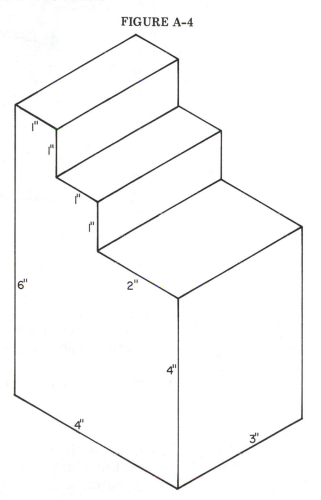

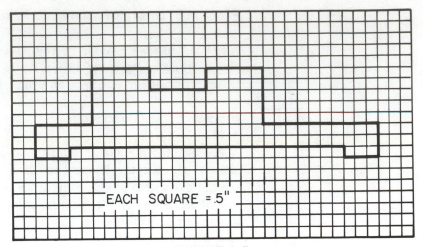

FIGURE A-5

FLOOR PLAN

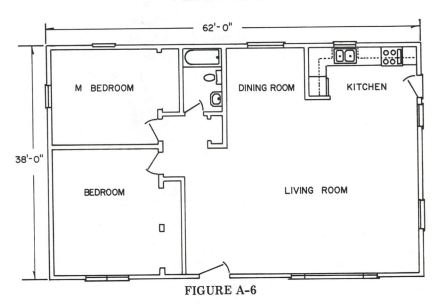

FIGURE A-6

Problem 8: Corrections Exercise

Manually draw a full-scale top, front, and right-side view of the object in Figure A-7. Digitize your drawing and display it on the CRT screen. The checker has determined that all dimensions are short by $\frac{1}{2}$ inch. Make all necessary corrections.

Problem 9: Mirroring Exercise

Figure A-8 contains a three-dimensional drawing of a symmetrical object. Manually draw a full-scale front view of the object. Digitize the left half of the front view and display it on the CRT screen. Add the right half of the front view by using the mirror command on the CRT keyboard.

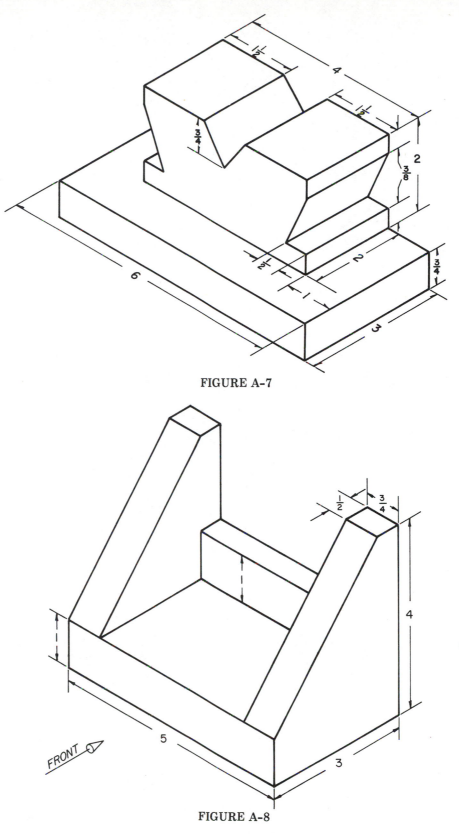

FIGURE A-7

FIGURE A-8

Problem 10: Overlaying Exercise

Digitize the walls on the floor plan in Figure A–6 and display this on the CRT screen as one layer. Then add all dimensions, room designations, and notes as a second layer. Command the plotter to plot an original drawing of the first layer by itself, the second layer by itself, and both layers at once as a composite.

INDEX